# YOUR
## *Wedding*
# ASTROLOGER

### How to Plan the Perfect
### Wedding Based on Your
### *Zodiac Sign*

#### KAREN CHRISTINO

**ADAMS MEDIA**
NEW YORK  LONDON  TORONTO  SYDNEY  NEW DELHI

**A**adamsmedia

Adams Media
An Imprint of Simon & Schuster, Inc.
57 Littlefield Street
Avon, Massachusetts 02322

First Adams Media hardcover edition December 2018

ADAMS MEDIA and colophon are trademarks of Simon & Schuster.

For information about special discounts for bulk purchases, please contact Simon & Schuster Special Sales at 1-866-506-1949 or business@simonandschuster.com.

The Simon & Schuster Speakers Bureau can bring authors to your live event. For more information or to book an event contact the Simon & Schuster Speakers Bureau at 1-866-248-3049 or visit our website at www.simonspeakers.com.

Interior design by Sylvia McArdle
Interior images © Getty Images

Manufactured in the United States of America

10 9 8 7 6 5 4 3 2 1

Library of Congress Cataloging-in-Publication Data has been applied for.

ISBN 978-1-72140-023-2
ISBN 978-1-72140-024-9 (ebook)

Contains material adapted from the following title published by Adams Media, an Imprint of Simon & Schuster, Inc.: *Your Wedding Astrologer* by Karen Christino, copyright © 2009 by Karen Christino, ISBN 978-1-59869-630-1.

# Dedication

*For my husband, Adam, whose heart, brilliance, and soul
spin round my life like celestial spheres.*

# Acknowledgments

Many thanks to Christopher Renstrom for his editing skills,
Renée Randolph for her astrological research, and Diane
Cramer for her medical astrology work. A big thank-you to
Sandy Choron for her unflagging enthusiasm. I owe a debt
of gratitude to Abby Strauss for piquing my interest in the
astrology of weddings, and to Frederick A. Margolin, Esq.
for his support.

I'd also like to thank the editors of *Modern Bride*, *Your Prom*,
and other magazines who gave me many opportunities to
focus on the topics of marriage and relationships. They include
Antonio van der Meer, Laura Himmelein, Betsy Goldberg, Anita
K. Henry, Kara Corridan, Michaela Garibaldi, Christina Boyle
Cush, Andrea Chambers, Mary Sears, Susan Schneider, Brenna
McLoughlin, Patricia Canole, and Sarah Eisen Nanus.

# Contents

# Introduction

Congratulations—you're getting married! Almost as exciting? You have astrology on your side to help make all that planning and decision-making easier than you could ever imagine.

When you align with cosmic forces, you gain a clarity you may not have thought possible. Wondering how to deal with your fiancé, parents, future in-laws, old friends, and forgotten relatives all at the same time? Astrology can tell you what to expect and how to handle everyone with grace! Trying to choose flowers, food, dresses, and music? The planning is practically done for you with astrology on your side. And don't forget the honeymoon! Just check the stars for the perfect location.

Astrology can help you sort through the hassles and make sure you come out ahead. We all have natural talents and abilities, as well as personal weaknesses. Knowing your Sun sign's strengths can help you put them to better use, and understanding your potential limitations will aid in working through them. And Sun signs aren't all there is to astrology; the Ascendant, Moon, and other astrological factors make us complex individuals. If you know your rising sign or your fiancé's Moon sign, check these out, too, for additional information and ideas to make everything even easier.

Part I: For the Bride is designed to make wedding planning as stress-free as possible. You'll find ideas designed specifically for your birth sign and insight into your own needs and desires to keep you feeling calm and focused. Astrology also suggests flowers, gems, locations, and types of honeymoons to help you brainstorm or narrow down your choices so you'll never feel overwhelmed.

Want to know more about your fiancé? How about your in-laws? Need help choosing a maid of honor or clueing in to what she's best at? Part II: The Groom and Others offers insight into your significant others. You'll discover more about their unique individuality and learn to love them for who they truly are.

Astrology is also one way to choose the perfect wedding date! Astrologers have been choosing auspicious dates for millennia. You can select a more favorable wedding date with the Appendix: Your Wedding Day. If you've already chosen a date, you'll find ways to utilize some potentially capricious astrological energies and get them to work for you.

Astrology's insights and understanding will help you feel more connected to the cosmos as well as your new partner. You'll learn more about yourself, your relationships, and your wedding day. With astrology on your side, you're sure to set the stage for wedded bliss!

# A Note to the Reader

Weddings have become more creative—and more inclusive. Not everyone wears a floor-length gown or tuxedo, but most still celebrate their union with variations on traditional themes. Astrology can help with these too. I've used the terms "bride," "groom," "his," and "her" with a nod to tradition and for easy reference. But Part I of this book can be used by any wedding planner—male or female, youthful or mature. Similarly, Part II's husbands and maids of honor can be read for any partner or attendant.

The classical male and female archetypes of astrology are complementary opposites and don't specify gender roles or sexual orientation. Aries is an active, pioneering masculine energy, and Pisces is an introspective, responsive feminine energy, whether or not they identify as male or female. The astrological characteristics of each zodiac sign are far broader than traditional suggestions of male or female behaviors.

Part I

FOR THE
*Bride*

# CHAPTER 1

# Aries

## (MARCH 21–APRIL 19)

Like the ram that races to the mountaintop first, Aries enjoys leading, starting new projects, and moving eagerly ahead. There's a wonderful simplicity to the Aries personality. You truly believe in the strength of the self. You're quick to react and have great decisive abilities. You will never "sit on the fence" and will jump over one as soon as you possibly can. Completely unselfconscious, you take action in an instinctive manner.

Because you need to rely on your own judgment and act accordingly, you dislike any restrictions to your progress; the Aries ram would rather lead the herd than follow. As a bride, you're the star of the show, so you're in the perfect position to take charge!

## WEDDING PLANNING

Aries is a fire sign ruled by the planet Mars. Both of these add to your high energy, courage, and need for excitement and stimulation. Active and assertive, you'll love the lively adventure of wedding preparations. All Ariens need to be physically active, and most Aries women will prefer to hop in the car and take a quick drive to the florist or printer themselves.

You're a forceful individual, and you need to direct your abundant energies toward your wedding goals. You'll be happiest when you can make your own decisions. Parents or in-laws who try to restrict you could feel the sting of your anger. You'd rather pay for the wedding yourself than tolerate interference from others who want to take control. You must be able to chart your progress and move forward with your plans without too much delay.

You need to share your thoughts and feelings with others—to talk, bounce ideas around, and just have a good time. Enlist your fiancé, family, and bridesmaids to help, and you'll find the camaraderie, appreciation, and acceptance from those you know best. You're naturally competitive and will also appreciate the opportunity to compare your progress with another bride's!

Ariens are spontaneous, active people who are not the most comfortable with long-range planning. If you're stalled in the middle of writing an invitation or selecting bridesmaids' dresses, talk to others who've been successful in their wedding planning who can lend advice from experience. You'll want to move forward on your own, but discussions can help you realize in your own head what's right for you. At the same time, you'll gain invaluable advice from those who've already been there.

Plunge right in, but don't overdo it. Focus on things like invitations, menus, and flower selection one at a time to avoid burnout. And be sure to enter your next "to do" on your calendar, or you'll risk blowing it off or forgetting about it altogether.

If your ideal gown doesn't present itself immediately, you may be tempted to take the next best thing, just to keep moving. Don't give in to impatience! Ask yourself, "Is this how I want to remember my wedding? Do I want to show my kids photos of this dress?" If you have doubts, it's best not to leap in just yet. A gown search can be tedious business, but if you keep looking, you'll probably find something that truly suits you.

You Ariens know you're capable of handling most tasks, regardless of whether you've done them before. While you may be tempted to forgo a rehearsal of the ceremony, just do it! Everyone needs a run-through to avoid standing on the wrong side or saying the wrong thing.

Your excitement may cause you to fidget, pace, or move about too much while you wait to talk with the baker or photographer. You can be impatient and restless, so bring someone to talk to or have your smartphone on hand to occupy yourself and to center your mind.

Don't get too impatient and leave in a huff if you must wait. Qualified vendors are often busy, and even good businesspeople can run from twenty to thirty minutes late. Don't be insulted, aggravated, or angry at these realities. If you have somewhere else to go, inform the right person. You may be bumped up or rescheduled. And if you've kept yourself occupied and relaxed, the waiting period will go faster and you'll be more confident and collected.

Learn to discuss your needs with your fiancé and the caterers, rather than shouting, "You're all jerks!" and storming off. You may feel that the solution is to do everything yourself, but trusted bridesmaids and family members can lessen your stress and increase everyone's enjoyment.

## STRESS-FREE!

You love big projects but may be frustrated by all the details and delays that crop up. If the bank's drive-through window is closed or you have to stand in line at the jewelry store too long, stress can mount. You're so active and energetic that you may also be careless of your health, especially when you're busy juggling a job and wedding planning with your fiancé, family, and friends. You could develop headaches, eyestrain, acne, sinus problems, or insomnia. Other typically Aries symptoms include bumps and bruises. Slow down and take a break! You may strain your muscles, so get help lifting heavy objects (like all those gifts!), especially when you're tense.

Regular exercise is likely to help you calm down and let off steam. Take a walk, do some kickboxing at the gym, or sign up for an aerobics class. Be sure to make time for some activity, as it will keep you balanced. Yoga or walking meditation can soothe your mind and body. Acupressure, a facial massage, or even a face mask should all help release stored tensions.

## LOOK GREAT!

Your dress should be both bold and beautiful. You'll look terrific in sleek sheath dresses with spaghetti straps or a halter top, which show off your dynamic style and high energy. You might enjoy a more casual look or a pants-inspired style. You have the edge and modernity to carry off metallic-colored shoes or a cuff bracelet with ease. You'd love to include a shot of bright color (perhaps a vivid Aries red!) at your waist, on some chunky jewelry, or on your nails and lips.

Your active, busy lifestyle doesn't leave much time for a complicated beauty routine, even on your wedding day. You prefer a simple regimen to zip through with no stress or bother. Since you're always on the move, you'll want a no-fuss hairstyle and makeup that can stand up to the rigors of an active day. And you'll scream if you're trapped in the stylist's chair when you have better things to do!

Since Aries rules the head, you may want to have an elaborate veil or show off some hair ornaments like barrettes, combs, beads, or gems. Keep extra hairpins and a headband nearby in case that great 'do drops from all the activity!

## A PERFECT AFFAIR

You're a casual, lively person and would like an affair to reflect your relaxed attitude. Morning or daytime ceremonies are more suitable for Aries than evening ones. You'd prefer a simple and even brief ceremony with vows that are direct and to the point.

Outdoor receptions should appeal to your fiery nature. You might enjoy a public garden, a ski resort, or a hilly area with a terrific view of the countryside. For cooler weather, you may be attracted to old inns with blazing fireplaces. You love to surround yourself with all your many friends, so find a venue large enough to hold them all.

Aries relates to the military, so a military wedding might be suitable if you or your husband-to-be has served. Boisterous or edgy themes strike your fancy, like the Fourth of July (with fireworks), safari, or rock 'n' roll. And to keep your adrenaline flowing and help everyone have a great time, be sure the beat goes on with music pumping the night away.

### Aries Flowers

Coxcomb, gerbera, honeysuckle, red carnation, red rose, tulip.

### Aries Gems and Stones

Amethyst, diamond, garnet, red jasper, ruby, white coral.

### Aries Colors

Flaming hues; brilliant reds; magenta, claret, carmine, scarlet, black, white, orange, yellow; anything metallic.

## ARIES HONEYMOONS

You'll adore active trips that include something risky, different, or adventurous, like whitewater rafting, surfing, bungee jumping, kayaking, or rock climbing. Or you might like to spend a week at a working ranch.

### Aries Cities

Bloomington, Indiana; Charleston, South Carolina; Daytona Beach, Florida; Raleigh, North Carolina; Springfield, Illinois; Wichita, Kansas; Wilmington, Delaware.

### Aries Countries

Chile, Guatemala, Ireland.

## LOVE AND SEX

For you, love is exciting! You're not afraid to make the first move, but if he doesn't respond, you'll just shrug your shoulders and move on to another activity. You're frank and open and will share exactly what you feel. You don't like playing the traditionally feminine role and will stick with men who are competitive with you.

You're bold and daring, and you take a no-frills, no-nonsense approach to life. Fiercely independent, you're a strong believer in equality between the sexes. Although you're passionate and sensual, asserting your identity can sometimes be more important than your desire to connect with your partner.

Love for you is fast and free of formality. You express your exuberance through your physicality. You've craved excitement from an early age and probably began sexual experimentation sooner than other girls. Sex is important to you for the self-gratification and release of physical energy and tension it brings.

### Great Aries Dates

Speeding down a mountain road on motorcycles, biking, Rollerblading, sharing a fast dinner or a fast car will leave you wanting more.

## SUCCEEDING AT LONG-TERM RELATIONSHIPS

You're a lively person who needs to stay in motion. Marriage must allow you a certain amount of spontaneity and freedom, as you won't let yourself be subservient to anyone. It's essential that you keep up with your career, your pastimes, and your pals (be they male or female!). You understand that marriage involves compromise, but if you can go Rollerblading or cycling as you're used to, you'll be thrilled. You'd love it, though, if your husband joined in.

Aries is the sign of the pioneer, and besides having the capacity to enjoy beginning your lives together, you'll inspire the two of you as a couple. Your optimism will encourage your new husband to be his best. You can also enthuse him through your powerful self-expression.

You Ariens are doers and like to see the tangible results of your work. When you've got a task, whether it's fixing the toilet or furniture shopping, your energy is inexhaustible. You'll always cut to the heart of any matter and get things done efficiently, regardless of whether your husband helps out.

Your temper may get the better of you at times, but you usually just need to let off steam in order to be yourself again. It can always help to share your feelings. Avoid escalating problems, however, by rehashing them again and again. Seek out solutions to disagreements that crop up on a regular basis by talking things out or setting up new arrangements. Your husband may not understand if you have an outburst. Try to control your voice, as well as what you say. After you've cooled down, a relaxed discussion can smooth things out—but make sure you've cooled down first! Another shouting match could easily occur if you get yourself worked up again.

You may want to tell everyone just what you think of your husband when you're angry. Don't ever allow yourself to! Telling family and neighbors too much may backfire on you and create hostility. Save your most honest and candid statements for your closest friends.

You can jump to conclusions as well, so don't be afraid to admit when you've made a mistake and raised your voice when you shouldn't have. Your husband will appreciate your honesty and candor.

When properly directed, your energy can't be beat. However, some Ariens jump too quickly into projects. Make a conscious effort to pause and reflect before you take action. Consider all possible outcomes before you put down a deposit for a cruise or pay for a dozen tango lessons.

As you Ariens always live in the now, you may abandon projects that take too long to accomplish or impulsively redirect your energies in another direction. No one will be happy if you leave the deck half stained or force your husband to finish wallpapering the bathroom all by himself. When you start a large project, break it up into many different parts. Set small hourly or daily goals toward achieving your overall objective.

It's best to remember that most people aren't as frank and candid as you are. You're direct about what you want and need, but many others, especially Scorpio, Cancer, and Pisces people, will only use indirect methods to get their ends accomplished. Your sincerity will get beyond tendencies like these in your husband, but you can benefit from trying to understand his point of view. Encourage discussion if he's not so clear-cut, and attempt to see what he really wants. You'll live more comfortably with him if you realize how different he may be from you.

Keep an open mind in discussions and don't let yourself get too perturbed. Try to listen more to what your mate has to say; you may find his input of value. Avoid being bossy and controlling, especially if he's weaker than yourself personality-wise. Not everyone exists at your energy level, but all have different perceptions, skills, and ideas to offer if encouraged.

You can be impulsive in financial matters, and this is often an important consideration in marriages. When possible, get input from your husband or devise checks and balances to keep from overspending.

## SHARING YOUR THOUGHTS WITH THEM

- **Aries:** Who's on first? "Me!" "No, me!" For maximum marital connectivity, when it comes to conversations, learn to take turns.
- **Taurus:** You talk, he doesn't. Strike a compromise between your eloquence and his reticence by learning to understand his unspoken language.
- **Gemini:** Your creative impulses blend well with his mental acuity. A magic synergy allows you to complete each other's thoughts, sentences, and ideas.
- **Cancer:** He can be thin-skinned; you can be blunt. He'll hear your stronger messages better if you're sure to say them sweetly.
- **Leo:** Both open and inspired, your heart-to-hearts will be like the best poetry: truthful, passionate, and illuminating.
- **Virgo:** You're a font of volatile verbiage; he's concise. He can help you get a handle on what you really mean.

- **Libra:** You have a good cop/bad cop partnership. With his diplomacy and your directness, you'll get to the truth of any matter.
- **Scorpio:** You're both strong-willed and strong-minded. But remember, long after you've let off steam, your sensitive Scorpio may still be simmering.
- **Sagittarius:** You're lively, he's engaging; together you exchange stimulating new ideas all day and party late into the night.
- **Capricorn:** You may not concur on all issues, but if you practice patience and he has faith, you'll learn to happily agree to disagree.
- **Aquarius:** His unique outlook and novel ideas intrigue you, and he values your enthusiasm and ardor. Your conversations are pithy and provocative.
- **Pisces:** You think in the here and now; he's got his head in the clouds. Bring him back to earth with questions about your (and his!) favorite things.

# CHAPTER 2

# Taurus

## (APRIL 20–MAY 20)

Taurus is symbolized by the bull. Think about one left quietly alone in a field, and you have an accurate picture of the Taurean personality: calm, serene, and relaxed. You enjoy the simple pleasures of life, take most things in stride, and don't get too easily excited.

You Taureans are by nature practical, down-to-earth individuals. You're extremely security-conscious and enjoy domesticity. And you seem to have a knack for attracting money and material wealth; is it any wonder that the term for an optimistic stock market is "bullish"? Not surprisingly, you're attracted to the finer things the world has to offer. You're sure to put together a lovely affair and enjoy all the comforts of married life.

# WEDDING PLANNING

Your Sun sign gives you a tendency to resist change. It may seem like a chore to begin your wedding planning, so snap out of that inertia! If you've definitely decided it's time to get married, begin your planning in some small way. Getting together with your and your fiancé's parents or checking out bridal registries online are both easy first steps.

Your present lifestyle of sleeping late on weekends, spending time shopping, or just hanging out may appeal to you more than making the effort to look for a catering hall or choose a photographer. You'll be better off once you're in a purposeful and regular routine. Make the decision, take the initiative, pick yourself up, and get going!

One important point for Taureans is setting a budget. Your taste is impeccable, and you're no doubt planning on a gorgeous affair and the stability of a long-lasting union. You know the value of money, how much you or your folks can afford to spend, and what's worth the investment. While you always admire the lush and plush, as long as you stick with your budget you'll come out fine in the end.

Don't give in to extravagant impulses. You certainly don't want to scrimp on your wedding gown. But if you splurge on your absolute ideal, you could break the bank. Control your budget by checking out designer knockoffs or hiring a seamstress to make your dream dress a more affordable reality.

Don't limit yourself by stubbornly insisting on having it all, though you'll probably get most of what you want through your strength of will and determination. But if you've decided on a large and elegant affair, be prepared to pay for it. If a designer dress is important to you, you may not be able to afford top-shelf liquor. Set your priorities. Decide what's most important and be prepared to cut corners in other areas. Otherwise, be ready to spend a great deal of time searching for attractive but reasonable bouquets, for instance.

You're a hard worker and will follow through on your plans. You have a natural ability to go after exactly what you want and will not swerve or falter along the way. Your purposeful attitude will ensure that you make progress with every effort.

Capitalize on your patience and persistence by committing a set amount of time to your wedding planning each day or each week. You can use this time in any number of ways: researching current trends, conferring with your bridesmaids, visiting vendors, or scheduling appointments.

Allow yourself the time to make a thoughtful decision. Don't let a jeweler pressure you into making a commitment to rings or bridesmaids' gifts immediately. Use your grace of manner to let her know what your reservations are; you may get a better deal.

Be certain to negotiate exactly what you want in terms of dress alterations, price, and number of fittings before making a commitment to buy a gown. Be aware of the telltale signs of a successful business as well: cheerful and relaxed employees, a neat and attractive workplace, and sufficient staff.

Spend some time at your prospective venues; atmosphere and environment can mean a lot. If you feel comfortable in a place, you'll feel better about the ceremony and affair as a whole. And once again, if you have reservations, bring them up right away. Six months from now it will be harder to secure more comfortable chairs than it will be today!

Celebrate your tolerant, patient side; it'll help you sail through things like meeting your in-laws that would shake up less stalwart souls. Keep up your usually calm pace and attitude, and you'll savor every step of the process.

## STRESS-FREE!

You're so single-mindedly determined to accomplish your wedding goals that you may ignore aches and pains. Tune in to your body! Not even Taurus is immune from the occasional pre-wedding tension headache. Get your fiancé to massage away the stiffness in your neck and shoulders. Or better yet, take a break from any craziness and escape to a spa.

You can typically suffer from a sore throat, congestion, vocal strain, and even ear infections. When symptoms arise, get more rest and stop pushing yourself so hard.

Light an aromatherapy candle or do some stretching exercises to relax. Practicing slow neck rolls should help to reduce tension. A walk in a park or wooded area could take your mind off your current concerns.

Shopping for dresses, visits from relatives, and considering a wine list are all pleasurable pursuits, but they may throw you off your usual routine. Try to keep up with the regularity of your life when you can. Cooking healthy meals should also help you connect with your more placid side.

Taureans love to eat, and you could overdo it if you're feeling stressed out. Avoid too many sweets, carbohydrates, or junk foods. Reach for fruits, whole-grain breads, or veggies instead.

## LOOK GREAT!

Touch is your strongest sense, and you're attracted to elegant, high-quality clothes that feel great against your skin. An off-the-shoulder or strapless gown in a soft fabric will show off your figure. Be sure nothing pulls or binds! Comfort is important to you, so take your time at the bridal salon and be sure you can walk, sit, and eat in that big dress!

You love textures and natural fibers and have an instinct for quality. You're the type who can save money by buying off the rack or at a discount store, as you recognize the look and feel of quality instinctively. Avoid chunky jewelry and strong perfume unless you're consciously going after a creative or unique style. Your best features are apt to be your soft, warm eyes, even brows, and thick curling lashes. Play them up! You'll want to rely on favorite products to do so.

Taurus rules the throat, and you appreciate timeless beauty, so try a vintage cameo, choker, or your grandmother's favorite pearl necklace.

A natural girl, you can't do without lip balm to keep your lips kissably soft and mints or chewing gum so your breath stays as fresh as you look.

## A PERFECT AFFAIR

You have an innate grace and refinement and can easily make great creative choices for your wedding theme and décor. The hall is sure to be tasteful and decorated with muted tones. You'd prefer a smaller guest list of close family and friends to a larger group that could get out of hand.

Your love of nature may prompt you to marry in a botanical garden or park. You wouldn't mind a formal or traditional wedding, but you'll want to keep it romantic. This might include a ring ceremony, personal vows accenting love and commitment, or the reading of a favorite poem.

You appreciate a relaxed atmosphere and would prefer that the music be soothing, like a string quintet, soft rock band, solo harp, or guitar. Rich gourmet foods are high on your list, but be sure there's something available for all tastes. A sweet, fruit-filled cake or individual desserts complete your special day.

### Taurus Flowers

Apple blossom, columbine, daffodil, daisy, forget-me-not, larkspur, lilac.

### Taurus Gems and Stones

Alabaster, carnelian, emerald, jade, moss agate, rose quartz.

### Taurus Colors

Pastels or earth tones; any shade of blue; pink, moss green, coral, other easy-on-the-eye shades.

## TAURUS HONEYMOONS

You always want to be comfortable and appreciate familiar surroundings. You'll be willing to spend more for something special, like a sensual spa or private bungalow. Or you might go for complete relaxation at a romantic inn.

### Taurus Cities

Billings, Montana; Durham, North Carolina; Gary, Indiana; Kansas City, Missouri; Las Vegas, Nevada; Miami, Florida; Montreal, Quebec; Newport, Rhode Island; Portland, Maine; Reno, Nevada; Santa Barbara, California.

### Taurus Countries

Ecuador, Ireland, Israel, Monaco, Portugal, Tanzania.

## LOVE AND SEX

You're sensual and sensuous: cuddling, kissing, or just holding hands with your man will make your day. Extravagant and indulgent, you keep your lover satisfied with good food and drink. You're turned on by a warm, inviting environment and consider it the perfect ending to a date to be entwined in a hot tub with champagne and caviar or curled up on the couch. You'll revel in someone who'll massage you with scented oils and explore your every erogenous zone. You have an instinct for what makes a man happy.

You become deeply attached, so avoid becoming possessive or jealous. You think, "He's all mine," but he'll need to have some space for friends and family, even women who are friends.

You need to take your time with sex and should always indulge in plenty of stroking and foreplay. You know what you like and will stick with it for maximum pleasure. But you and your husband could get into a rut! If he wants to vary things, try to take his lead. Or check out books, magazines, and videos for some fresh ideas.

### Great Taurus Dates

Mellow and relaxed times are your best bets. Try country music or oldies concerts, or a three-course meal at a romantic restaurant.

## SUCCEEDING AT LONG-TERM RELATIONSHIPS

You're a faithful and reliable partner to your mate. Practical and responsible, you'll work hard to create a secure union. Security for you involves both a solid emotional foundation and tangible assets. You have a great instinct for money and finance, understand the value of things, and love to surround yourself with the luxury of fine clothing, furniture, food, and all the best that life has to offer.

Money usually becomes an important issue. You need to earn enough between the two of you so you can buy the things you want and those that make you feel most secure: a comfortable home, warm and attractive clothing, and good food. The lush and plush will always appeal to you. You'll find it most relaxing and soothing to live in a gorgeous home with a terrific view and soft music in every room. If you can't afford it yet, you'd appreciate a man who helps with creating a soothing environment on a budget.

Your pleasant personality and natural good manners make you an asset to any mate. He was probably attracted to your quiet courtesy, sweetness, and good nature. Your ability to bring beauty and harmony to your living atmosphere will help both you and your husband feel more comfortable.

All Taureans should live in a calm and pleasant atmosphere. You'll deal with difficult personalities, complex situations, and emergencies with the same practical and unruffled outlook that you bring to everything else. While you can put up with a lot, regular doses of noise, shouting, emotionality, and undependability can frazzle you. This type of environment will eventually take its toll on your emotional as well as physical health. Seek instead to encourage a more friendly and relaxed atmosphere, or be sure to carve out quiet time alone to unwind.

You'll always prefer a strong structure and regular schedule. If your husband is the type to do things on the spur of the moment or to change plans at the last minute, you either need to adapt or get him to adjust his habits—perhaps a little of both. Taureans like and need familiarity and stability, and you'd eventually find too much change on a regular basis to be emotionally draining.

Your greatest asset is your determination and dedication to your goals. You'll single-mindedly pursue them with patience, persistence, and tenacity. You have the ability to work on your marriage and will not be swayed by difficulties or obstacles in your path. These will simply serve to make you more committed to your life together. As a realist, you know what will or won't be possible.

You have a straightforward outlook and are honest and truthful. You can be trusted to keep your word and will safeguard confidences. Because of your constancy and integrity, you'll provide an extraordinarily solid base for both you and your partner.

Your opinions are strong, and you'll stand up for what you believe in. This is a great asset, but on occasion it could create friction. Try to be reasonable if you disagree with your husband. No matter how strongly you feel, remember that you may have to compromise in the long run.

Some Taureans become obstinate and stubborn; you should avoid this in your closest relationship. Try to learn the give-and-take needed in a close connection. While you may get what you want by forcefully demanding your own way, you could damage your relationship. You should also try to be aware of constructive criticism. Your husband may have different ways of looking at things and could help you to improve yourself. And even though you don't like to change the way you usually do things, if you think practically, there's always room for improvement.

Especially in these high-tech times, you also need to get used to change about you. Don't freak out if your husband wants to buy a new computer or big-screen TV on a regular basis! Try to be adaptable to this type of behavior if you're generally happy with your life together.

All Taurus people need plenty of rest in order to function best. You'll be a better partner when you feel refreshed and relaxed. Make sure you don't skip meals, either. A good breakfast of protein-rich foods or whole-grain cereals will keep you going through the toughest morning. While you Taureans have strong physical constitutions, you can easily wear yourself down by neglecting proper sleep, nourishment, and relaxation. Put these on your priority list, especially in times of stress.

If you ever find yourself becoming bored, chances are that you've fallen into a rut. Plan some unique outings with your husband. Set about making some improvements to your home. If you are still feeling indifferent, take some more initiative. You must assert yourself if you need to change things.

## SHARING YOUR THOUGHTS WITH THEM

- **Aries:** His assertive communiqués help you transform your warm and fuzzy gestures into hot and heavy expressions of love.
- **Taurus:** Both your minds are attuned to a relaxing wavelength. You'll need no words to communicate that this soft, sweet sofa-stint is forever.
- **Gemini:** He knows how to jump-start your mental motor while you steady his motor mouth.
- **Cancer:** It's hard to say which one of you is sweeter! Keep the love lines buzzing with honeyed words and sugary sentiments.
- **Leo:** The great value of your mutual stubbornness is the steadiness of your commitment. Accept that you sometimes speak different languages, and savor a foreign tongue.
- **Virgo:** You both see things clearly. You insist on the truth, and he tells it precisely. Vital ideas flow freely between you.
- **Libra:** Both committed to collaborating peacefully, you enjoy nothing more than thoroughly airing and sharing your intimate thoughts.
- **Scorpio:** He may not always say all he feels, as you do, but you can be sure he feels it just as strongly.
- **Sagittarius:** He says what he means a dozen different ways, while you think before putting it succinctly. But you both value directness.

- **Capricorn:** Neither of you shy away from examining the bottom line or telling it like it is. Quite a constructive combination!
- **Aquarius:** You're very personal; he's more philosophic. For maximum harmony, be sure each understands the other side of the duet.
- **Pisces:** Your realistic grounding balances his imaginative understanding. Spill your hearts, and misunderstandings will be rare.

# CHAPTER 3

# Gemini

## (MAY 21–JUNE 20)

Castor and Pollux, the mythological twins, are the name-sakes of the two bright stars in the constellation Gemini. Think of a pair of twins who have grown up sharing every-thing. Each chatters away, always has a companion, and is totally comfortable in the other's company. This is how an individual Gemini acts with others: open, straightforward, and communicative.

Geminis enjoy talking, learning new things, and exchang-ing ideas with others. Friends, relatives, and associates take the place of the missing celestial twin. Geminis often need to seek out the company of others in order to feel whole. Your wedding will give you many friends, new experiences, a sense of celebration, and fun—all your essentials!

# WEDDING PLANNING

Geminis can do anything. Your vivaciousness and humor will give everyone around you a lightness of spirit. Since you are by nature a communicative type, you should start your wedding planning by talking. Share your plans with whomever you run into in the course of your busy day. You probably have quite a large circle of friends and acquaintances, and you'll find many ideas and recommendations simply by asking around.

Use a mass email to speed things up. Get in touch with prospective vendors, friends, relatives, acquaintances, coworkers...anyone you can think of who may be able to give you ideas or information. Your search should also include local bridal magazines and newspapers. Skim the classified and advertising sections to get an idea of what's available. The key is to collect as much information as you can—a little information leads to more. If you're persistent and follow up on all leads, you'll develop a wide pool of possibilities. It helps to seek out as many possibilities as you can. Out of a dozen ceremony sites, only one may be right for you.

Take advantage of your multitasking skills. You can do three things at once: write a thank-you note, listen to a demo tape of a band, and taste test a wine. Make a lot of appointments. You'll have fun meeting new people, learn more about many different organizations, and possibly get some more leads. In a short time, you're sure to find the perfect registry or DJ! And remember, if you said you'd call your maid of honor or future mother-in-law—call her. This is no time to procrastinate.

You should also look for situations that give you the ability to interact with others. Whether it's discussing the guest list with your parents, shopping for a gown with your maid of honor, or getting a consultation on your hair and makeup, others around you will provide needed stimulation and interesting ideas. You should be able to use your communicative ability and quick-moving mind, and this is one of the best ways of doing so.

Most Geminis have highly developed nervous systems, and many can be high-strung. You could become overwrought or exhausted by too much of a good thing. While you need a stimulating atmosphere full of people and ideas, too much stimulation will give you the negative influence of feeling "wired." No one can keep moving all day long, and you should always vary your day with rest periods and breaks. Take some time to settle your mind. If you begin to feel scattered, yoga and breathing exercises should help you feel centered and refreshed. Don't try to do everything at once but break things up into shorter projects. In the excitement of a hectic day you'll probably forget about reserving time for yourself. Make an effort not to.

If you can, find a quiet and calming place in which to focus and work. Noise from neighbors or idle chatter from family members and friends can distract you from the important task at hand. Your concentration may be shattered by the smallest of intrusions. Seek out a private room or office for quiet time when you need it.

You're such a free spirit that as the big day approaches, the idea of such a huge commitment may start to rattle you. Make time for a great date to talk it over with your fiancé or best friend, and you'll feel better.

## STRESS-FREE!

Naturally high-strung, you may become scattered by the demands of too many obligations and activities, leading to tension. Though you usually love company, houseguests or even too much time with friends might cause you to eventually feel overwrought or jumpy. Gemini rules the nervous and respiratory systems, and tension can show up in these areas. You may tend to suffer from anxiety, worry, allergies, and even asthma when you're feeling wrung-out.

Cutting caffeine will help you calm down, and don't smoke! Deep breathing should help center you. Your preference for a variety of activities could lead you to weight lifting, stretching, aerobics, or work on a treadmill to help you relax. Skating, power walking, and tai chi are other possibilities. Reflexology work may also calm you down.

Any activity that takes your mind off your preoccupations can be a plus. If you do journal writing, painting, or needlework, these can all distract you. Even ordinary things like cleaning, grocery shopping, gardening, or watching your favorite sitcom may help, as they keep you diverted and focused on everyday tasks. Be sure to set aside time for relaxing activities when you're feeling wrung-out or scattered.

## LOOK GREAT!

Sometimes you're made up; sometimes you prefer to go au naturel. You're a mercurial character and enjoy variety in your life. You may want to change outfits at some point during the reception or adjust your makeup for a more dramatic look as the evening goes on. Geminis love mixing things up, so a hairstyle with a swept-up front and loose or long back suits you well. Or try a white gown with touches of color in delicate velvet bows.

You may see 101 gowns that you think would look great but may not be able to decide exactly which to wear! Before you freak out, try a two-in-one outfit, like a dress with a matching jacket or wrap to suit your mood. You're attracted to the funky and irreverent. Keep it light and bright, and you'll be on the right track. Featherweight, airy fabrics attract you, as do shiny silks and satins. Don't buy a large or heavy gown, which could overwhelm your personality.

You're stimulated by the many little ways to complete your look, like flowers in your hair, rhinestone barrettes, lots of rings and bracelets, even a hairpiece or gloves. You might enjoy trying out a change of hair color or adding extensions or a hairpiece for your wedding. Just be sure to start experimenting long enough before the big day to leave plenty of time to change your mind!

## A PERFECT AFFAIR

Geminis are versatile. You can pull together a wide array of people, styles, and activities to make your wedding work. Generally not sentimental, you may prefer a civil ceremony or opt for both a civil and religious one to suit your dual nature. No matter what else, your wedding must be lively and fun. Invite all your friends and family and have as many attendants as you can. A casual buffet afternoon or a cocktail reception might suit you, but you wouldn't mind if the celebration extended over an entire weekend. Think about a backyard tent, a park picnic lunch, or a country-club tea party.

Your vows are likely to be quite important to you. You may want to write and read your own vows or customize a favorite song or poem. If there are children in your life, consider working them into the ceremony as a ring bearer or flower child.

### Gemini Flowers
Azalea, baby's breath, goldenrod, lavender, lily of the valley.

### Gemini Gems and Stones
Beryl, blue aquamarine, blue zircon, clear quartz crystal, sapphire, yellow topaz.

### Gemini Colors
Bright colors; lemon yellow, hot pink, lime green; soft tones of blue, gray, green, and violet; multicolored florals; tiny prints.

## GEMINI HONEYMOONS

New and interesting places always intrigue you, so go somewhere that will stimulate you intellectually that gives you many places to see and visit. You might like to take a road trip or join a tour group, stay at a golf resort, go on a cruise, or visit a tropical island.

### Gemini Cities

Anchorage, Alaska; Annapolis, Maryland; Berkeley, California; Concord, New Hampshire; Fresno, California; Indianapolis, Indiana; Louisville, Kentucky; Memphis, Tennessee; Niagara Falls, New York; Salem, Oregon.

### Gemini Countries

Denmark, Egypt, Georgia, Italy, Morocco, Norway, South Africa, Sri Lanka, Tunisia.

## LOVE AND SEX

You're witty, bright, and friendly, and you love to flirt. As you're outgoing and interested in many things, you need a man who's your intellectual equal. Priorities are open communication and mental stimulation.

You dislike feeling hemmed in by a mate; he must allow you the freedom to be yourself and do your own thing. You can be casual and are easily able to handle multiple relationships with a variety of people. You're exciting and stimulating, always on the go. Too much routine and regularity will bog you down.

You need to have variety in love, which could mean dressing up, a new 'do for a special evening together, or being sure he stays out of a rut romantically. Your ideal is a lively, intelligent dude who enjoys double dating or hanging out with your friends.

Having a playmate in both the sexual and entertainment venues is also a must. You relish romance novels and now and then an erotic movie or book. Phone sex can raise your libido. Sometimes you can be casual about sex or will sublimate your sexual drive by staying busy. In fact, constant activity can leave you breathless and may be almost as exciting as sex.

### Great Gemini Dates

You like to stay on the go, so a trip downtown, to the mall, or to a party or new restaurant are all tops with you.

## SUCCEEDING AT LONG-TERM RELATIONSHIPS

Your adaptability and flexibility are perhaps your greatest assets in any relationship. You can adjust to changing situations, the demands of a mate, or simply fluctuating circumstances. You don't worry when plans must change as you find new situations stimulating and challenging. You'll be intrigued and not turned off by a man who changes his mind. Preconceived notions or old ways of doing things don't hold you back. And you like to experiment with new ways of accomplishing things, simply because they're mentally stimulating.

You enjoy discussion, examination, and trial and error until you come up with an ideal solution. Keeping the lines of communication open between you will always be helpful. Your often-brilliant, logical, and quick mind will easily offer any number of clever alternatives to any dilemma, and you can function well in brainstorming sessions. Realistic and objective, you'll dispassionately review a problem on an abstract level in order to come up with the most intelligent course of action.

You'll easily try out suggestions from your husband and have no prejudices about what will work before you think things through. You're decidedly not an egotist and won't let yourself become involved in power struggles or bids for competition. You'd prefer to remain on an equal, friendly footing and to consistently enjoy a pleasant and caring relationship.

You're very quick and often have a highly developed sense of humor. You can add lightness to many situations. You're witty, charming, likeable, and easy to be with. You handle people with diplomacy and can influence your husband through discussion, quick answers, and the ability to see and understand both sides of a question at once. Through your personal ease, inventiveness, and finesse, you can soothe an angry mate and reconcile differences.

Stick to the facts. Don't take rumors or gossip as truth, especially if it involves your husband. Your discussions can be so fluent that you may have a tendency to expand on the facts or imply more than is true. While this is an asset to good storytelling, it's not good for developing trust and confidence in a relationship. If decisions based on your thoughts aren't founded on simple facts, they could backfire on you. Stick to the plain, unadorned, boring truth!

Hopefully you've found a partner who gives you a certain amount of freedom. Don't overdo it, though. You can inadvertently scatter your energies by hopping back and forth around town from friends to errands to haircuts, and so on. Don't ever let socializing get in the way of your primary relationship. Plan joint outings with your husband from time to time instead.

If you need to spend more time with your husband at home, there are endless diversions. Today's world of technology can provide you with many ways of reaching others elsewhere while still sharing an evening with him. Use your smartphone, email, or blogs to communicate with others while you stay put.

Because you seek out the new and are totally alive in the present moment, you can become forgetful or unpunctual. Don't let other things distract you on your way to important appointments with your husband. Keep an eye on the time; pick up an agenda book or use your smartphone to keep track of your appointments. Train yourself to consult your schedule often each day and jot down notes or reminders. Organize and plan your time.

You speak quickly and can promise the Moon to your husband before you've really thought things through. More serious types could find you fickle if you do! Try to keep your word and follow through on promises. After the numerous events of your busy day, you may not recall whether you really said you'd pick up dinner tomorrow or not. Write down important promises and remember to consult that list. Or ask your husband to remind you with a call, note, or visit. If a task is that important to him, he'll follow up.

While money is not of the greatest importance to you, you should learn to use it effectively. Dealing with money on an abstract level is easy; it's the practical experience that may throw you. Once again, a journal can help. Keep track of all expenses by jotting them down. Don't overuse your credit cards and always get receipts. If you can train yourself to consistently do these simple things when spending, you're sure to stay on top of money matters and enjoy both a balanced checkbook and a balanced relationship.

Don't overwork. Many Geminis suffer from stress and nervous tension. Overwork can lead to crankiness and arguments. Take a break, enjoy a day off, or plan a long weekend together to relax away from your cares regularly.

# SHARING YOUR THOUGHTS WITH THEM

- **Aries:** You're so mentally stimulating together that yesterday's argument is easily outshined by today's witty, lively, loving discussion.
- **Taurus:** When your thoughts get scattered, you'll appreciate his consistent sense of direction. You help him consider other viewpoints.
- **Gemini:** Two bright chat-a-holics, you give new meaning to the phrase "oral gratification." Talk your way to ecstasy!
- **Cancer:** Your intellectual riches are a match for his sensitivity. You'll intrigue and enliven each other.
- **Leo:** Your charm meets his fire; you intoxicate each other with laughter, lively conversation, and spirited love letters.
- **Virgo:** You both shine brightly with wit and intelligence. You'll profit from his ability to focus, and he from your multifaceted interests.
- **Libra:** Sharing your feelings comes naturally as your flexibility and his facility with words make for great confabulations.
- **Scorpio:** You're lively, and he's deep. You can brighten his moods; he'll help you center.
- **Sagittarius:** You both have a vibrant need to learn and share. Your mutual charisma helps you explore complex new concepts with each other.
- **Capricorn:** Your effervescent conversations keep him from overdosing on obligations. When your nerves get jangled, he'll help calm your thoughts.
- **Aquarius:** You share a mutual open-mindedness. His original outlook sparks your curiosity and vice versa.
- **Pisces:** Opposites attract! He'll help you see the mystical and magical. You'll get him to be clear and logical.

**CHAPTER 4**

# Cancer

## (JUNE 21–JULY 22)

Cancer the crab is ruled by the changeable Moon. Your moods and feelings are variable; Cancer is a sensitive and responsive sign. You are often imaginative, creative, and ambitious—but in a quiet way. And yes, you can be "crabby" when you're hurt, when things aren't going your way, or just because of a bad mood.

Young crabs can grow new legs to replace those that have been damaged or lost, and Cancer, likewise, has the ability to keep on moving forward. You are a tenacious and persistent person and adaptable to circumstances. Yes, you may complain and retreat into your shell at times. But you'll slowly and effectively work your way onward toward your wedding goals.

# WEDDING PLANNING

Your warm heart thrills at the thought of bringing your greatest guy and your whole family together to celebrate your happiness. Surround yourself with supportive people who care. You're a sensitive soul who may wilt without extra love and affection at this emotional time. Be sure your bridesmaids are people you know well, those you can confide in and count on, and avoid pushy or annoying individuals.

Whatever your wedding goals or ultimate dream may be, you Cancerians should think about an affair you'd be comfortable with, something you'd feel you can handle without too much stress or anxiety. You're very much in tune with your inner feelings and a situation that doesn't feel quite "right" to you, for whatever reason, will likely remain that way.

Take it slow and easy. You'll probably have high ambitions for your wedding, but we all have to start somewhere. Cancer people can dwell on the past and may be inhibited about starting something new. You often feel diffident about making changes in your life, even when looking forward with excitement. You may also feel ill at ease in calling prospective wedding planners or photographers. You can circumvent this by first doing research online, in local newspapers, and in bridal magazines. You'll then have a better idea of what you want and need and feel more confident.

Ultimately, you'll have to face those personal meetings. Because you can be shy and retiring, you may feel a little apprehensive. Lighten up the burden of feeling that an interview is an "all or nothing" situation. It's only your attitude and point of view that will change. Perhaps you can have a nice phone conversation with a few florists beforehand, going over the basics and your needs. Or take your mom or maid of honor to the bridal salon when shopping for a dress. If you follow these steps, you won't feel like you're going into the meetings totally "cold" or alone. You'll also find that you're more prepared, relaxed, and knowledgeable.

It's good to speak with a number of different vendors to compare prices and services. You will get used to it! And you'll soon find that you're asked a similar set of questions each time. Cancerians can usually profit from being a little pushier than they think they should be. Though you might feel insecure, you should nudge yourself to speak up and voice any questions or concerns.

Your instincts and impressions will be a big part of your decision-making process, so put them to practical use. If it's possible, try to come back to the catering hall on more than one occasion, for instance. Or use your time waiting to observe the surrounding atmosphere. Visit the actual spaces where you'll have your ceremony and reception. Could you see yourself as part of this environment? Would you feel comfortable and at ease here? These are some of the important questions to ask yourself before making a decision.

You may want to involve your family in the ceremony. Agree on their roles in advance. Young men can be ushers, parents may give special readings or say prayers at the ceremony, and you can make vows to children from previous unions.

Above all, try not to get worked up over every little conflict! You are extraordinarily responsive to the moods and feelings of others, but you need to take a step back and avoid getting drawn into potential mini-dramas and meltdowns. If your little brother says he's not coming if he has to wear a corsage, turn the issue over to your dad. And when the pressure builds and you feel like running away, go for a drive or watch a funny movie like *The Wedding Planner* or *My Big Fat Greek Wedding*.

## STRESS-FREE!

Cancer is very protective of the emotional self. If you're having any difficulties, you can benefit from rest and a change of scene; a break from routine may brighten your spirits. Cancer is a water sign, so you can relax with a bath, a swim, or a visit to a lake.

Your emotional sensitivity may lead to mood swings and anxiety if you are upset. Try not to build things up in your mind or dwell on them negatively. Cancer rules the stomach, so digestive problems could follow as well. You may have a tendency to overeat and might especially enjoy comfort foods like ice cream and cheese. Try not to overdo it, especially if you're feeling tense or worried; it will agitate your system even more. But cooking or baking a cake might nevertheless soothe jangled nerves.

Even a good cry can freshen you psychologically by releasing your feelings. You'll also benefit from simple physical movement as you may have a tendency to become listless and rooted in one place. Go out for a walk, do some stretches, or just engage in some physical activity like cleaning out your closets or organizing your dresser drawers to get your energy flowing.

## LOOK GREAT!

Your emotional sensitivity extends to your skin, so treat it with care! You'll look best in natural-looking products, which allow your warm glow to shine through. Be sure to test-drive your makeup in advance to avoid possible slip-ups. And use a foundation with SPF if your affair will be out of doors.

You love dreaming of the past, and vintage-style fashions with lots of skirts in organza or crinoline reflect your romantic side. You may actually want to look for a vintage gown. You'll flip over a 1950s-style design with a circle skirt and fitted top. Cancer is ruled by the Moon, so silvery or shimmering fabrics, off-white, or antique white should appeal to you. Grandma's ring, your mother's dress, or an heirloom cameo show your attachment to your family. Cancerians love to be feminine, so don't forget the intimates! A fancy bra or teddy will make you feel sexy and sophisticated.

Comfy is happy, so be sure your dancing shoes are low enough to boogie and that you can move in that gorgeous gown—wear it in advance so you know nothing pinches or binds. Your evening bag should not be overstuffed. But you may want to leave room for your smartphone so that you can take some photos to save, savor, and share the memories! Add an extra pair of pantyhose, just in case.

## A PERFECT AFFAIR

Most Cancerians seek intimacy and privacy; you may want to choose a small church ceremony with only your close friends and immediate family in attendance. You'll feel best with an officiant you know well and can probably get him or her to travel to your ceremony site if you choose.

Your home is the center of your universe, so why not consider a reception there? Since Cancer is a water sign, other choices include halls or resorts near lakes, rivers, or brooks. Or take over a seaside restaurant for a day.

Your family is important to you, and you may want to involve them in the ceremony. Parents or close friends can offer a prayer, blessing, or reading of your choice. If either you or your partner has children from a previous marriage, you might also want to include them in the ceremony. Children can also hold rings or the bouquet, or walk with the bride or groom.

### Cancer Flowers
Delphinium, hydrangea, iris, larkspur, patchouli, water violet, white rose.

### Cancer Gems and Stones

Milky opal, moonstone, pearl, selenite, white onyx.

### Cancer Colors

Smoky colors; opalescent and iridescent hues; silver, smoky gray, pale or sea-foam green, silvery white, pale blue, antique silver, peach, cream.

## CANCER HONEYMOONS

Cancerians are tied to the home, so you might not want to go that far away. If you travel, bring sentimental mementos with you. You love being near the water, so a private bungalow on the beach or traveling to Mexico, Hawaii, Tahiti, or Niagara Falls might suit you.

### Cancer Cities

Boise, Idaho; Eugene, Oregon; Fargo, North Dakota; Green Bay, Wisconsin; Minneapolis, Minnesota; Omaha, Nebraska; Providence, Rhode Island; San Diego, California; San Francisco, California.

### Cancer Countries

Argentina, Bahamas, Canada, Madagascar, Romania, Seychelles, Thailand, United States, Vietnam.

## LOVE AND SEX

You're warm and supportive and will show your nurturing side in loving and caring for your partner, cooking him a meal, or helping him shop for new suits. Your strong need for a mate reflects your overall desire for emotional closeness. You're ready to meet his every need, sometimes too much so as you have a tendency to mother your husband. In return for your comfort and care, you expect to have your own emotional needs met. If they're not, you could become moody or clingy. Try to lighten up and put on a smile for that special someone—you'll even convince yourself to have a better time!

You're not afraid to be smothered with warmth and affection, and you need a demonstrative sexual partner who'll kiss you deeply and cling to you tenaciously. With your passion for food, you feel great satisfaction in preparing and sharing a meal with your partner.

Family is important to you, too, and you'd prefer a devoted partner who welcomes children and will embrace the responsibilities of family life. A desire for children might heighten your sexual responsiveness.

### Great Cancer Dates

Try snuggling together with a bowl of popcorn to watch a movie, or sharing a luscious dessert at an outdoor café or coffee house.

## SUCCEEDING AT LONG-TERM RELATIONSHIPS

You're a domestic gal at heart, and you crave a warm home and family. You need to maintain good connections with your relatives and ideally with his as well. Stay in touch with your mom, dad, and siblings. Take the time to share meals and weekend dates with your new husband, and you'll have the makings of bliss.

Finances are also important. If you can't manage to pay your basic household expenses plus put a little away for a rainy day, you'll feel anxious, pressured, and stressed. Both you and your husband need to be aware of how much you spend each month and how much you earn. You'll never take unnecessary chances and will be a cautious spender. You instinctively know how to hold on to and use money. You should be the one to handle finances if you have a less fiscally responsible spouse!

Cancer is all about security. You easily commit yourself to being a wife and will strive to make the relationship last. Your home and children are also important. Hopefully, you've already discussed these issues with your fiancé. If not, it's time to address them! You'll probably want a comfortable home of your own one day, and children as well before too much time goes by. Be sure you agree on these goals and how to achieve them.

Decorate your space with things you enjoy. Pictures of family and home, plants, and even soft music can make you feel at ease in your environment and more comfortable with your partner. You have a rich emotional life and a knack for knowing just what your husband wants and needs. You generally rely on instinct and feelings to help you make decisions, and know deep in your gut what's right for you. But because of a tendency to go along with others to avoid stress, you may take the easiest way out of a problem or acquiesce to your husband's decisions. You could also follow the line of least resistance in your goals and might ultimately end up with a partnership that doesn't meet your needs. Listen to your instincts when something doesn't feel quite right. And try to step outside your feelings from time to time to get a more objective view of your situation.

You're very sensitive and may be insecure, often having a hard time asking your husband to do favors or help you out. Encourage yourself to be more assertive about what you want; you might have to shake things up a bit to do so!

Always try to take criticism objectively and not personally. Most others are not as sensitive as you are, and people usually don't mean any harm when they speak brusquely or bluntly. Take this to heart particularly with Aries, Sagittarius, or Scorpio husbands. Cancer is ruled by the changeable Moon, which can make you moody at times. Don't take upsets, PMS, or anger over other issues out on your husband! He's your most intimate connection. Share your feelings with him, but also find creative pursuits that make you feel good and distract you from annoyances. Dancing, journaling, getting out to the movies, escaping to a lake or seashore, or having lunch with a good friend can all center you and uplift your spirits. Finding a rewarding job or career, even if it's only part-time, should also keep you feeling centered and strong.

It can benefit all of you Cancerians to see the bigger picture and to view your own place as part of the team, not just subjectively. You could become like the hermit crab and close yourself off from your husband when you're upset. Consciously keeping the lines of communication open and maintaining a positive attitude about working through any relationship issues can improve on this trait.

Conflicts are generally not resolved on their own no matter how you may try to avoid them, and your husband could become hurt if you close yourself off when the chips are down. Whether your own concern is getting him to put the toilet seat down or making time for a date night, avoidance will only compound your problems over the long term. You love him, so give him the opportunity to help you by sharing your feelings and concerns.

If you're ever feeling unhappy, remember to try to be realistic. You may tend to exaggerate your feelings and imagine the worst when you're emotionally drained. Try not to build things up in your mind. And don't just sit back and hope things will change. Cancer people are emotionally drawn to the past; you like to save and collect things that remind you of past events. Remind yourself of your love for your spouse by spending some time with your wedding album or video. Then be assertive and take action to work things out with your husband.

# SHARING YOUR THOUGHTS WITH THEM

- **Aries:** His bluntness is merely his style; it doesn't mean you need to forgo your softer, sweeter fashion. Don't take offense at his frank expressions.
- **Taurus:** In this cozy partnership, your private language needs no translation. You both wear your hearts on your sleeve!
- **Gemini:** You may feel shy, but if you express your dreams and yearnings, his rationality can help you plan a path to accomplishment.
- **Cancer:** You're both softhearted and sensitive and appreciate words of support, sympathy, and reassurance.
- **Leo:** When you let him think he's the star of the show, you'll both be known for expressing yourselves with warmth and ardor.
- **Virgo:** Your emotional truthfulness and his elegant expressiveness combine for a compassionate connection.
- **Libra:** If you appreciate his objectivity, and he your subjectivity, you'll express yourself more gracefully, and he'll emote with more empathy.
- **Scorpio:** You prefer indirection and he likes suggestion; a bit more directness at times can increase the voltage.
- **Sagittarius:** Your candy-colored words collide with his candor. He can speak without thinking, but you'll never need to question his truthfulness.
- **Capricorn:** You're both sensitive but may not share your concerns easily. Over time, caring and support make for a dynamically informative duo.
- **Aquarius:** You speak from your heart, he from his head. But your responsiveness and his idealism combine to get your messages across.
- **Pisces:** You both intuit exactly what the other is thinking and feeling. Your romantic natures express themselves best in tranquil settings.

# CHAPTER 5

# (JULY 23–AUGUST 22)

Leo lionesses have big hearts and childlike qualities. Have you ever watched kittens in a pet-store window? They hold your attention because they're inventive, fun loving, and can come up with 101 uses for a scratching post. So can Leos. Your creative inspiration and dramatic flair make you dynamic planners. A little self-absorbed? Yes. But when Leos lose themselves in a project, there's a lot of energy directed in a positive manner.

Like the lion, you're confident and dignified. There's a vital, strong will in the Leo nature as well as a great deal of pride that constantly seeks to prove itself. You respond well to challenges, are courageous, and love to lead and be in the spotlight. Your wedding is your biggest show to date!

## WEDDING PLANNING

Your wedding not only showcases your devotion to your fiancé; it should also allow you to indulge your party-animal side. You're very good about keeping your sights on future goals and will endeavor to achieve them. This works very well for your wedding, as you're able to focus your attention over an extended period of time.

Seek out brides who've had terrific weddings, or read about a celebrity who's done exactly what you dream about. Use their examples to help you plot your own course. Leos are great at taking chances and using initiative. After you've done your homework and some soul searching, you'll probably find it easy to spring into action.

You love being in control and know how to delegate authority. Once you've chosen your bridesmaids' dresses, you might want to put your maid of honor in charge of the fittings. Or get your fiancé to focus on the travel plans after you select your honeymoon destination together. Consider hiring a wedding consultant. You may not have the time or inclination to do everything yourself and will get expert advice on all the details from start to finish.

You'll always shine in the spotlight. Your dress is one of the most important elements of the entire affair. You'll love looking forward to your appointment, shopping with your bridesmaids, and having the undivided attention of the saleswomen at the bridal salon. But you should also consider having a gown made just for you. You can create your own perfect look and might even save some money in the process.

Leo is one of the most creative signs of the zodiac, and you'll express your personality through your choice of musicians or a DJ. Take your time to listen to a number of them before you make your choice—for Leos, only the best will do! You'll want an elaborate, over-the-top affair, but not everyone can afford 500 guests and the best catering hall in town.

To make the wedding extra special, choose a theme and plan around it. Whether it's sentimental, reflects your ethnic or cultural background, or capitalizes on the season, you're sure to create an especially memorable event and give your special day a fun and creative twist.

You'll look back on your first dances for the rest of your life. Be prepared by selecting songs and rehearsing with your dad and fiancé. If you really want to shine, think about taking some dance lessons or hiring a choreographer—there are many studios that specialize in weddings.

Email your local and city papers, alumni news, and any other periodicals you think appropriate to find out how to submit your engagement photo and wedding announcement. Start at least a month before the wedding. Submit to as many as you can to guarantee inclusion and follow up if you don't get a response.

This is a time you'll remember forever, so be sure to indulge yourself. Invest in the best products for your skin and hair at least a few months before the wedding. Get a facial or massage when you're feeling stressed. As the wedding draws near, it may be time for a spa getaway alone or with your bridesmaids.

Don't allow your assertive streak to take over. You may be center stage, but this is not a solo show. Remember that you're there to share this special day with those you love; keep their needs and feelings in mind. Be sure your maid of honor is comfortable with scheduling your manicure or hair appointments, and give your fiancé plenty of time to pack by gently reminding him of the hours remaining 'til your honeymoon.

## STRESS-FREE!

You're a creative powerhouse and want to bring all your incredible ideas to light. But you may have a tendency to overextend yourself or do too much. Though you're thrilled to be getting married, it's a major life change that can create stress. You could have a weakness for back and shoulder strains and stiff muscles. Yoga, tai chi, or stretching exercises will gently help you release tensions. Or put on a playlist of your favorite songs and sing along.

Left unchecked, stress in Leos could potentially lead to heartburn, high blood pressure, or palpitations. Pace yourself! You don't need to do everything alone. You are good at delegating tasks, so get your fiancé, bridesmaids, and parents to help out if you're feeling fried.

In warmer climates or for summer affairs, you could become over-heated or be prone to sunburn. Wear plenty of sunblock if you'll be out of doors for any period of time, and keep those sunglasses on. Avoid too much physical activity in hot weather, and drink plenty of fluids.

## LOOK GREAT!

This is your big day, so go for maximum impact. You're a true diva who knows how to look your best and be the star of the show. And this is prob-ably one of the only times in your life that you'll have a legitimate reason to wear a train or a tiara!

You've probably fallen in love with dresses in bridal magazines and cat-alogs. Now's the time to see if they stand up in real life. You can be at-tracted to designer looks but could probably find knockoffs that look just as good at a cheaper price. Or sharpen your fashion designer instincts to create your own designer dress. Go as dramatic as you dare, with long, body-conscious styles and attention-grabbers like Swarovski crystals, glitter, and spangles.

You'll probably prefer having your makeup done by a professional for this once-in-a-lifetime event, but don't neglect trying it out first in the proper lighting to judge the effect. And don't forget that gorgeous Leo mane! Whether you pile it high on your head like a princess or leave it down in long, lush curls, you'll be sure all eyes stay on you!

## A PERFECT AFFAIR

Plan a fabulous processional and make it last. You'll shine in a receiving line, so take your time there too. You may not have the opportunity to connect with everyone again during the reception. Don't omit a stretch limo to take you to your destination in style—this is a little luxury that you're sure to savor.

Leos are natural performers; if you're musical, you might like to sing a special song as part of the ceremony or reception. And of course you'll want to enhance the party atmosphere with the best band or DJ you can find! Choose lively dance music so you and your guests can let loose and boogie.

You have a terrific creative imagination and may be stimulated by thinking about having your ceremony or reception at a concert hall or theater, in a dance hall, at a castle, solarium, or at the edge of a forest.

### Leo Flowers
Dahlia, heliotrope, marigold, peony, poppy, rosemary, sunflower.

### Leo Gems and Stones
Amber, carnelian, citrine, fire agate, orange topaz, red obsidian, ruby, tiger's eye.

### Leo Colors
Yellow, orange, gold; other rich and shimmery shades.

# LEO HONEYMOONS

Go first class all the way! Spoil and indulge yourself for this once-in-a-lifetime event. You may enjoy the urban nightlife of big cities like Las Vegas or New York, going to a casino, or staying at a guest castle in Europe.

## Leo Cities

Baltimore, Maryland; Butte, Montana; Cheyenne, Wyoming; Chicago, Illinois; Colorado Springs, Colorado; Juneau, Alaska; Milwaukee, Wisconsin; Sacramento, California; Tucson, Arizona.

## Leo Countries

Bolivia, Cyprus, Jamaica, Liechtenstein, the Netherlands, Singapore, South Korea, Switzerland.

# LOVE AND SEX

You're loyal, warm, and generous, and you'd do anything for the man you love. You have a sincere and candid nature, so your husband will always know where he stands. You love the drama and glamour of romance and appreciate flowers, gifts, and other tokens of affection. You enjoy going out to parties, concerts, or the theater with your husband.

You're in love with love, and the excitement of a planned tryst heightens your erotic impulses. Sex is important to you, as you need it to feel good about yourself. Sharing a monogamous relationship boosts your self-esteem, but you're also excited by casual flirtations and flattery. You're turned on by expensive displays of affection.

Proud and flamboyant, you take great pride in showing off both yourself and your husband. Your requirements for a love connection include creativity, admiration, and lavish doses of loving. Continuing a sense of being courted by your mate with flowers and gifts offers you the excitement and romance you crave. You'll get a thrill when he opens doors, picks up the concert tickets, or just takes you to the dentist. But you'll seem like a prima donna if you expect it all the time.

Great Leo Dates
Getting dressed up for special occasions like anniversaries, birthday parties, or weddings really thrills you.

## SUCCEEDING AT LONG-TERM RELATIONSHIPS

Without laughter and a generous dose of romance in your life, you tend to feel unfulfilled. You're happiest when you're active, sharing the excitement of a movie premiere, dining at an exotic restaurant, or going on a snowboarding weekend with your husband. Dress up and indulge your theatrical urge to feel like a celebrity. Unforgettable outings will keep your marriage fresh and spontaneous.

You'll be at your best when you're inspired by a sense of excitement. As philosopher Joseph Campbell put it, "Follow your bliss." If your husband doesn't enjoy going to softball games, hosting your nephew's birthday party, or catching the latest romantic comedy release, pursue these activities on your own or with friends or family members.

You have a healthy ego and simply need to know that you're esteemed and appreciated. Most Leos enjoy recognition, commendations, or praise from their significant others. You can live without it, however, if you receive the ultimate rewards: shared respect and unconditional love.

You're frank and direct and will express exactly what you feel. No one intimidates you, and you'll speak up if you feel you're being treated unfairly. Your husband will appreciate your candor and respond in kind. You readily admit your own mistakes with honesty and take action to correct them.

Be conscious, though, that others could potentially find you too bold or competitive. Husbands of a quieter nature might be put off by your upfront expressions of strength and determination. You're quite powerful, and some could find that you come on too strong. Try to be aware of the way your husband responds to you. Don't always be the one to make decisions, for example. Solicit his input and feelings whenever you can. You'll find that he responds better to encouragement and pleasantries than to being ordered about like a servant.

Your kind, generous nature gives you the ability to create intimacy. You genuinely like other people, and you make and keep friends easily. Others are attracted to your warmth and spontaneity. You give of yourself openly, and this can make you popular. All of these qualities contribute to your ability to make your marriage last; you're typically loyal and committed.

The sign of Leo gives a natural strength, endurance, and courage, so you have the ability to work hard and long at a relationship if it's ever necessary. A problem is only a challenge to you. You can inspire your husband with your positive attitude and enthusiasm.

Your kind, open nature may backfire at times. You can be manipulated, and you may be subject to flattery because of your own genuine sincerity. Does your husband always compliment you before asking you to take out the trash? Try to be aware of his behavior and your own response to it.

Leos sometimes promise more than they can deliver. Don't exaggerate what you're able to accomplish. Consider carefully what you can and cannot do before making any commitments, and make sure you follow through on all promises.

Your Sun sign might make you stubborn and sometimes opinionated. You have the ability to make up your mind quickly and will want to act on your decisions. Yet your husband will have his own opinions as well, and it may be necessary or diplomatic to discuss the issues and compromise. Don't force your judgments on him. If you present your arguments in a persuasive manner (one of your talents), you may be able to sway him to your side. Always treat the love of your life with kindness and respect.

Your sense of self-confidence may lead you to take necessary risks and make these successful. Some Leos, however, become foolhardy. They take too many risks with their own careers, money, or investments. This is gambling, pure and simple. And it's fun, which is why you might want to indulge in it! Confine yourself to prudent or necessary risks and especially avoid flirtations outside of your marriage.

You can also be impatient and, particularly in stressful or challenging situations, could lose your temper. While it might be appropriate occasionally to raise your voice to make a point you feel strongly about, do this consciously and in a dignified manner. Even when your husband is wrong, avoid a showdown! Opt instead for a low-key, sensible discussion or phone call.

The final and often fatal Leo shortcoming is laziness. If you find your household tasks boring or uninteresting, you may have a tendency to avoid them or force your husband to take them on. Infusing your chores with imagination will help you enjoy them more. Turn the mundane task into an event and take pride in whatever you do. Divide things up fairly between the two of you. He may not mind washing dishes if you do the more creative task of cooking.

## SHARING YOUR THOUGHTS WITH THEM

- **Aries:** He sparks your imagination, and you give him plenty of ideas. You fuel each other's minds!
- **Taurus:** Both sides of this couple speak up succinctly. But you each may have very definite ideas and need some give-and-take.

- **Gemini:** A lively and articulate couple, you'll chatter 'til dawn about nearly anything. Why sleep when you can shoot the breeze?
- **Cancer:** You're emotionally centered, and he's confidently loving. You both speak with warmth from the depth of your souls.
- **Leo:** You're a mutual motivational-speaker society, where heartfelt honesty and passionate pep talks inspire you both to courageous feats.
- **Virgo:** Your dialogues are strong on both style and substance. You focus on what's said, he on how to say it.
- **Libra:** He tries to be balanced in his opinions, while you're more forceful. Brainstorming together will lead to a productive interchange.
- **Scorpio:** You love to share thoughts, while he's more introverted. He'll trust your sincerity, and you'll learn circumspection.
- **Sagittarius:** You can laugh at the world together and inspire each other's craziest fantasies. You may shock the censor but not each other!
- **Capricorn:** You need to roar your love from the rooftops, while he writes about his in his study. Meet each other halfway—in the bedroom!
- **Aquarius:** You know you're often right; he doesn't think anyone ever is. When you entertain the other's point of view, you'll discover exciting new perspectives.
- **Pisces:** You're devoted to each other and will share thoughts best while having fun or in each other's arms.

**CHAPTER 6**

# Virgo

## (AUGUST 23–SEPTEMBER 22)

The Virgo symbol suggests someone with a job to do. It's a maiden holding an ear of wheat, but there are many more where that came from! Virgos are known for their hard work, dedication, and no-nonsense approach to life. You're purposeful and attack any project head-on. You recognize things of worth, know how to handle money effectively, and will put your effort into making the most of your circumstances, whatever they are. Always discerning, you know quality when you see it—whether it be in your fiancé or a diamond ring. The Virgo maiden has spent so many eons meticulously separating the wheat from the chaff that she can never be fooled by second best!

# WEDDING PLANNING

You're earnest and down-to-earth and will enjoy fine-tuning all the plans for your wedding. Remember that you have a lot going for you! You may be modest in assessing your value, but you can be an ideal planner. In your realistic attitude and your willingness to do what it takes to get a job done, you'll score points again and again. Your attention to detail is one of your greatest assets, so put it to good use. Follow all leads, leave no stone unturned, and don't dismiss any possibilities out of hand.

You're not easily fooled by flattery or romance and are one of the more pragmatic wedding planners. A wedding is a project like any other. Even though you're in love, honey-tongued salespeople will not sway you into spending more than what something is worth.

Your budget is key. Investigate the market for gowns, flowers, and caterers to get an idea of the going rates. Discuss what you can afford with your fiancé and parents. Then decide on your priorities. Are your favorite flowers more important than a designer dress? You can probably expect to pay less for a catering hall in your hometown than one in a nearby city. Rates are lower in the day than in the evening, and Fridays and Sundays are typically less expensive than Saturday affairs. You may be surprised at the cost of fresh flowers, even in season. Dried or silk flowers or bunches of wildflowers can be beautiful and help you save for something else.

You'll appreciate the efficiency of an online gift registry that is accessible to everyone. But your discerning eye will want to examine china and housewares firsthand. So choose a large department store that you can visit, and be prepared to set aside several days to make your choices.

Take your time to sample caterers' offerings, even though the companies may be highly recommended. You're quality-conscious and can discriminate between the many dishes offered. You won't choose something just because it sounds good!

Many Virgo women enjoy crafts projects, and you'll feel terrific when you add your own talents to your wedding. You might like to do calligraphy for your invitations, prepare the wedding favors, or even make your own dress. You'll save money, but these projects can also help calm your nerves if you're feeling frazzled.

You probably won't want to scrimp on photography. Find a photographer who'll give you the originals or negatives or a videographer who'll provide you with the complete unedited material that's been shot. You can then easily make copies yourself or have the video footage re-edited for a special gift or anniversary present.

A realist at heart, you know there are many business details that must be handled in addition to your marriage license. Insurance policies such as car, life, medical, and home or rental will no doubt need updating. Familiarize yourself with your own and your fiancé's policies and discuss what changes will need to be made. If you're changing your name, you'll also need to update your Social Security card. And visit your local bank to get the paperwork started to open up a joint account.

Don't stress yourself and blow things out of proportion. Little mistakes may tend to throw you. The stationer will certainly redo matchbooks with your name spelled correctly, and a dress shop can easily adjust your hemline. So don't fret—just handle it!

## STRESS-FREE!

You love things to be "just so" and strive to pull all the details of your wedding together. But you might be prone to worry or anxiety, even over minor issues. Try to keep things in proportion. No one will really notice or care if the bridesmaids wear shoes that don't exactly match their dresses! Consciously let it go.

For Virgos, stress can aggravate intestinal problems, food or environmental sensitivities, and allergies. Eating smaller meals might minimize these troubles. Eating regularly, chewing fully, and relaxing while you eat should all be of help. Plenty of fiber will be good for you—so tune in to the fresh fruits, local veggies, and whole grains you like. Avoid caffeine and alcohol. Herbal remedies, such as chamomile tea, can help calm you.

Exercise can also help, but don't overdo it. Cycling, hiking, or taking stairs should settle your nervous system down. Or take a long walk in a park or forest. Find some meditation or relaxation music and listen to it regularly. If you must worry, set aside a particular time to do it. By disciplining your mind in this way you'll worry less and be more objective in your fretting sessions. Follow up with some more relaxing activities.

## LOOK GREAT!

Virgos are down-to-earth. You'll want to find a clean, uncluttered look, including simpler, natural styles for hair and makeup. Try to eat right and get plenty of sleep and exercise in order to be at your best and minimize worry on your big day.

Bridal salons might order one size larger than your exact size to allow for alterations, but you'll want a perfect fit—and too many alterations could change the original shape or fall of a gown. Try on other styles from the same manufacturer to find out what your size should be, instead of taking a salesperson's word for it, and order that one. Alterations will then be minimal. Try out your hairstyle, go for as many gown fittings as you can, and walk a mile in those potentially unforgivable shoes.

Details like covered buttons, fine lace, and the perfect headdress attract you, and you can have all of these added to a simpler gown. Or consider a shrug or capelet for more variety.

For you, neatness is a must and less is more. Don't worry about pantyhose if you're marrying outdoors in warm weather—invest in a pair of fancy sandals instead. Perfectly manicured nails and a shimmering gemstone bracelet complete your look.

Don't forget to carry tissues, toothpaste, a toothbrush, floss, and mouthwash—you wouldn't dream of going anywhere without them!

## A PERFECT AFFAIR

Many Virgo women prefer a no-frills style—the opposite of what most people think weddings should be! You can keep your affair manageable, affordable, and even minimalist if you choose. You might prefer a civil ceremony with a judge, justice of the peace, or mayor. Having the ceremony and reception at the same site can also simplify things.

Think quality rather than quantity for guests, food, and even flowers. Serving desserts rather than cake can be a pleasant alternative. And breakfast or brunch affairs are usually simpler than large sit-down dinners and can be refreshing choices.

Virgos are often concerned with the environment. You may want to make your wedding more "green" by serving a vegetarian meal, including local flowers and produce, or wearing a handmade organic dress.

You're attracted to natural settings and would enjoy a ceremony or reception out of doors—in a garden, greenhouse, public park, or a beautiful open field. And, yes, you can have a flower-dog, but only if he or she is well behaved!

### Virgo Flowers

Buttercup, bouncing bet, chrysanthemum, Queen Anne's lace, sweet Cicely, sweet William, thistle flowers, violet.

### Virgo Gems and Stones
Agate, green peridot, hematite, jasper, sapphire, sardonyx, tourmaline.

### Virgo Colors
Anything speckled or spotted; dark brown, green, dark gray, navy blue, black, khaki, wheat, cream, yellow, pink.

## VIRGO HONEYMOONS

You're sure to plan your trip down to the last detail and get a great deal on your travel and hotel costs. Virgos like to learn things, so you should enjoy going to a museum, stargazing, or visiting a resort near nature and wildlife. Staying at a health spa will soothe your spirit.

### Virgo Cities
Boston, Massachusetts; Buffalo, New York; Fairbanks, Alaska; Idaho Falls, Idaho; Los Angeles, California; Toledo, Ohio; Winnipeg, Manitoba.

### Virgo Countries
Belize, Brazil, Costa Rica, El Salvador, Luxembourg, Malaysia, Malta, Mexico, St. Kitts, Trinidad and Tobago, Uruguay, Venezuela.

## LOVE AND SEX

You're serious and realistic in love, and won't put up with flaky or flighty men. You're a subtle and consistent lover and not afraid to try new things. As an earth sign, you have a natural affinity for the sensual side of life. But if you have any questions, a sex guide or manual can be extremely helpful. You're great at following instructions and will have your husband sighing with ecstasy in no time!

You appreciate the feel of fine fabrics like silk and satin on your skin. Quality lingerie and sheets can put you in the mood for love. You'll enjoy sharing massages or a hot tub together. Conversations about your mutual dreams and goals can even heat things up for you. With your passion for work, you may sometimes allow your career to become an aphrodisiac. But once you allow yourself time to relax, you can release all your tension into love and sex. Virgos are not usually indulgent, but a glass of wine or champagne should relax you and help make for a romantic evening.

### Great Virgo Dates

You're down-to-earth but also appreciate quality. You'll have fun picnicking at the park, walking in the woods, or having a special lunch at a fine restaurant.

## SUCCEEDING AT LONG-TERM RELATIONSHIPS

Above all, you need to feel a sense of purpose in your marriage. This could mean helping each other to reach life goals or simply collaborating on something as basic as gardening or refinishing a piece of furniture. As long as you and your husband are working together, you'll be deeply satisfied. Sharing your passions and interests together as a team appeals to you.

One of your greatest assets is your quick and able mind. Your thoughts are generally practical, and your logic and analytical abilities can easily be put to use to solve day-to-day problems. You're a realist, and your observations, deductions, and decisions are sound and accurate. You'll enjoy all types of discussions and conversations, especially about your day-to-day lives together. These help you feel more connected and secure.

Naturally curious to understand things, you'll rely on experience rather than the opinions of others. You like to make your own decisions, and you have the ability to make constructive criticism and suggestions for improvements. Yet you're not typically opinionated; you easily listen and adapt to your husband's ideas as well. This can lead to genuine cooperation and domestic stability.

You enjoy work with money and can bring accuracy and precision to bear on financial affairs; you get a thrill from balancing a checkbook or reconciling a bank statement. Your instinctive understanding of the effective use of money also helps stabilize your lives together. You're conservative in spending, know a good bargain when you see one, and seek maximum value for your dollar.

Perhaps your most important asset is your ability to work hard. You'll go about completing the most difficult tasks in the same way that you do everything else: by taking them apart into manageable pieces. You show great zeal in attacking a large project and seeing it through to completion. Your relationship will thrive if you share household decorating or repair projects, hobbies, cooking, or workout routines.

You're thoughtful and considerate, carrying out your responsibilities to the best of your ability. Your calm, patient manner will inspire your husband to feel reassured and secure. You're a kind and caring individual who always likes to help out. If your husband needs help getting ready for work and doesn't have time for chores or keeping up with the laundry, you're likely to take on these responsibilities and feel good about pitching in. But don't allow yourself to be taken advantage of. Be sure that there's a fair division of obligations within your marriage, or you could feel frustrated in the long run.

Your fine ideas and good sense of humor can always help to spice up your communications. In your desire to be purposeful, you may forget niceties of this sort and should consciously remember them. Take time out for dates, vacations, and relaxing weekends together. Saturdays are not just for chores! To fully enjoy your marriage, you've got to have fun too.

Your excellent sense of discrimination can aid in improving the quality of your life, but many Virgos may become overly critical. Picking on yourself can lead to low self-esteem, overwork, and anxiety. Remember that we can never reach true perfection on this earth.

You might also have a tendency to underestimate yourself. If you have doubts about your worth as an individual, focus on your assets rather than preconceived liabilities. We all make mistakes, but these shouldn't worry you if your attitude is positive. Speak up when you feel you're not receiving your due. You may feel shy about asking for more time together, but you won't remain happy if your needs are overlooked by you or your husband.

You can be prone to overwork and might exhaust yourself physically and emotionally if you're not careful. A well-rested and refreshed person is healthier. Plan and work ahead of deadlines when possible and leave your job concerns at work—don't bring them home.

Try not to criticize your husband too much. You may feel that he could do a better job, keep a neater bathroom, or get a haircut more often. He probably could, but your relationship will suffer if you consistently offer unsolicited advice. Always be constructive with your advice and opinions. Try to remember his good points as well as his shortcomings. Don't become a nag about small details. Many people are sensitive to critiques. If you must do it to improve domestic conditions, pick your battles, phrase suggestions pleasantly, and stay constructive and supportive.

Your rational outlook will help you realize when your relationship needs more work. Carve out some time for a heartfelt conversation in a relaxed setting. Airing your views can only help to get things back on the right track.

# SHARING YOUR THOUGHTS WITH THEM

- **Aries:** You think before you speak; he argues first and asks questions later. Moderate each other, and your domestic dialogues will be divine!
- **Taurus:** You love words; he speaks when he has something to say. You'll rev up his conversations, while he'll connect with your colloquy.
- **Gemini:** A dynamic talking duo! Your practical outlook grounds his thoughts, and his breeziness inspires you to fresh forms of expression.
- **Cancer:** He thinks with his heart; you solve problems with your head. You'll help him be more objective while he encourages your sensitivity.
- **Leo:** You want all the details, while he prefers figurative, flowery language. Concentrate on what he means, rather than how it's put.
- **Virgo:** Both of you are down-to-earth and simply spoken. Let go of a shared tendency to sweat small stuff, and you'll quickly grasp each other's thoughts.
- **Libra:** You're precise, while he likes to explore ambiguities. Help pin him down; he'll aid your objectivity.
- **Scorpio:** You're both subtle and analytic, able to reach solutions together. There's no puzzle the two of you can't solve!
- **Sagittarius:** He's a big broadcaster, you're better at small talk. He'll light up your thoughts; you'll curb his.
- **Capricorn:** You're both realistic, with work and responsibilities on your minds. Finding something more upbeat to discuss lightens you up!
- **Aquarius:** You're two reasonable, kind people. When you take the time to deliberate with your practicality and his idealism, you'll understand much.
- **Pisces:** You're a realist; he's a dreamer. If you hint at his forgotten duties, he'll help broaden the scope of your thoughts.

# CHAPTER 7

# Libra

## (SEPTEMBER 23–OCTOBER 22)

Charming, friendly people, Libras always seek beauty and peace. You're naturally refined, polite, and calm individuals who believe in the give-and-take necessary to make any relationship work. In their need to please everyone and see all points of view, Librans may end up indecisive and procrastinating. But once a real compromise has been reached with Libra logic, you can bet that all will agree it's fair, just, and impartial.

This sign has a love of beauty and the finer things in life. The exquisite taste exhibited by Librans can be seen in every facet of your lives. You'll create a lovely affair while keeping everyone happy.

## WEDDING PLANNING

Libras are partnership people who are most fulfilled when connected with others. Celebrate your union! Before you begin the details of planning your wedding, you should have already made some general choices regarding what type of dress, venue, and ceremony you're attracted to. Remember to seek balance and the golden mean consciously, whether it's between satisfaction and cost, distance to the reception and convenience, or your desires and those of your fiancé.

It will help you to work with others in order to feel your best. Your fiancé can give you strength, encouragement, and good ideas. Many men are not the most enthusiastic about wedding planning, but it's important to make your major decisions together. Issues involving the budget, ceremony, officiant, and type of reception should all be joint decisions. Let his own priorities and interests dictate how he'll be involved. If he's a music fan, have him handle the DJ or band. Is he a travel bug? Then he should make the honeymoon arrangements. If he's got a head for business, let him keep track of the budget and how expenses are adding up.

Sharing your own thoughts with others can help solidify them and give you objective insight. Trusted confidantes should be important members of your planning team. Your mom, maid of honor, bridesmaids, and a wedding planner can all help you clarify your own ideas and offer suggestions and opinions. A wedding in your own backyard may seem just as appealing as one in Aruba. Seek the advice of friends and family to help you pin this one down early. It may help to go back for another fitting or band demo if you're really in a quandary; bringing someone else along should help you decide.

Libras can be procrastinators; you like to have enough time to make important decisions. So start your planning early and keep up with it. Magazines and books about weddings typically offer planning schedules—get one and stick to it! You won't have the luxury of endless time to decide whether to book a particular band or order a certain cake. Don't debate too long.

Your generally charming, gracious, and refined personality is a plus in dealing with vendors, in-laws, and parents. You're usually self-possessed and express yourself well. You put others at ease with your intelligence and tact while commanding respect with your dignified demeanor. You know how to please others and are firm about keeping things running smoothly. A sweet "That's a good idea" will keep pushy individuals from getting too involved as you move forward with your own plans.

You have the diplomacy to handle divorced parents, squabbling siblings, and wistful bridesmaids with ease. You'll be able to finesse a seating arrangement that will keep everybody happy. But remember the old adage about not being able to please everybody all of the time. Don't readjust to everyone's needs. Your desire for harmony could have you making unwanted concessions. If you've decided it's an adults-only affair, don't let friends from out of town talk you into inviting their obnoxious ten-year-old; arrange for daycare instead. If your great-aunt Sheila wants to bring her pet Chihuahua, it may seem fine until he starts chasing the waiter serving cheese puffs. Use your deft diplomacy to just say "no" to special requests like these.

Finally, be sure to spend quality time with your fiancé. You'll often be talking about the wedding, but you should set aside afternoons or evenings when you do anything but. It's a time to celebrate your connection and make it stronger. It's not just about the event; it's about your relationship! Make that a priority at this time as well.

## STRESS-FREE!

A sense of balance aids all aspects of your life, but you're likely to be more active during wedding-planning times. Be sure to match this with plenty of rest and relaxation and make time for as much as you need. If people become emotional or angry it can throw off your system, so surround yourself with positive, peaceful, and supportive friends and family members.

Libra rules the kidneys, which can take the stress when you're feeling tense. Support them with plenty of liquids, and cut down on sweets and white flour. When your equilibrium is upset, you might also have skin problems—the bane of any bride! Plenty of greens and a sensible diet will help your body maintain its balance.

Exercise could help release tension, and you should enjoy tennis, golf, or ballroom dancing. Getting out in the fresh air, going shopping, updating your gift registry, or writing thank-you notes can all settle your spirits and return you to a more relaxed state. Or just sit back and divert yourself by reading a great book or watching a terrific movie.

## LOOK GREAT!

You have a wonderful sense of beauty and style. No matter what you choose, you'll look elegant and polished. You know how to showcase your grace and refinement and will look just right for any occasion.

Long and lean is a classic Libra look, so try a long satin column rather than voluminous skirts. Or consider skirts with light, airy volume. A designer pants suit or low-backed dress with beads, buttons, or bows would also suit you. You love luxurious fabrics, so now's the time to swathe yourself in them!

You're sophisticated and have the poise to pull off an elaborate updo with style. Libras look better with straight, sculpted hairstyles rather than "big hair." Take the time in the months before your wedding to experiment with a few styles along with your veil to be sure everything's perfect.

Invest in a great foundation to enhance your skin's natural glow. You can afford to wear more makeup than you usually do, as you ordinarily choose muted, soft tones. Complete your fabulous look with long gloves, silk or satin lingerie, faux jewels for your hair, and a classic scent. Powder, blush, and a delicate hankie in your bag will keep you looking great 'til 2 a.m.!

## A PERFECT AFFAIR

Your innate sense of style and elegance are sure to imbue anything you create with sophistication. You may prefer a formal or semiformal affair. A sit-down dinner or lunch suits your style. You might enjoy an outdoor reception, but if so, prepare yourself for the possibility of inclement weather.

Readings for your ceremony could include the Libra themes of love, cooperation, and collaboration. A special song or prayer that's meaningful to both of you should be included. You may prefer classic vows but can add some personal touches of your own.

You're sure to seat everyone to harmonious advantage, but go the extra mile with elegant or unique escort, menu, and table cards.

Libra themes include Valentine's Day, a garden party, a wine tasting, and Greek mythology. Or take your cue from a celebrity wedding that you admired.

### Libra Flowers
Bluebell, freesia, gladiolus, hydrangea, tea rose, violet.

### Libra Gems and Stones

Aventurine, chrysolite, emerald, opal, pink diamond, rose coral, sapphire.

### Libra Colors

Pastels and cloudy tints; bright, clear colors; pale shades of yellow and green; pink shades, soft rose, powder blue, mauve, yellow, amber, lavender.

## LIBRA HONEYMOONS

You love luxury and glamour, and this is the time to go for it! Book a four-star hotel and go out to all the fine restaurants you can afford. You might enjoy a wine tour of the Napa Valley or the East End of Long Island. A visit to the Taj Mahal, the monument to love, is sure to have deep meaning for Librans.

### Libra Cities

Albany, New York; Baton Rouge, Louisiana; El Paso, Texas; Knoxville, Tennessee; Las Cruces, New Mexico; Montpelier, Vermont; Orlando, Florida; Phoenix, Arizona; Richmond, Virginia; Santa Cruz, California; Yuma, Arizona.

### Libra Countries

Belgium, Botswana, China, Fiji, France, Germany, Guinea.

## LOVE AND SEX

You're a true romantic who loves the dating game, but you're happiest in a one-on-one relationship. You're not sappy or sentimental about love, but you'll be attentive, considerate, and cooperative toward your husband. You insist that your partner treats you as an equal in the bedroom. But you dislike confrontations; you'll always be ready to compromise and cooperate in order to reach greater intimacy.

You're more traditional than many in terms of lovemaking but will do much to accommodate your mate. Things that seem vulgar, coarse, or crude will never be on your favorites list, however. You enjoy foreplay and love talk.

Charming and sociable, you're turned on by luxuries and lavish events. The latest fashions make you feel sexy and desirable. Romantic vistas beguile you. You're truly in love with love and crave romance in your life. Candles, wine, piano bars, and dimly lit restaurants put you in the mood for love. Pampering yourself with a pedicure, blowout, facial, or massage makes you feel great about yourself and raises your amorous instincts.

### Great Libra Dates

You love being a hostess and should have a blast entertaining at home. Or try classy times at art galleries, the theater, a fancy club, or great restaurant.

## SUCCEEDING AT LONG-TERM RELATIONSHIPS

Libra is the sign of partnership, so you really crave a sense of companionship and cooperation in your marriage. Play to your strengths: your ability to hear his feedback, balance it with your needs, and rationally solve problems together. When you get stuck, draw on your special spirit of compromise. For example, if he's committed to staying in the same home, redecorating will give you a sense of change and movement.

You need to feel you're on an equal footing with your mate, sharing in the household chores or working together toward common goals.

Fairness is important to you, and if someone tries to take advantage of you, you won't hesitate to assert yourself.

You Libras always need to be able to work in cooperation with others. Everyone has unique skills, talents, and abilities, and you recognize that better results can be achieved when these are combined. Your husband may be a closet chef—let him exercise his talents while you handle the wine and dessert. If he likes to drive, you'll happily handle the map and be the copilot. Being alone for long hours will suppress your natural talents and could cause you to feel down or unhappy. Make sure there are opportunities for shared work and companionship. Arrange your schedules so you have as many evenings and weekends together as possible.

As you always strive for a sense of harmony and order, it's important that the atmosphere surrounding you at home be pleasant. You're sensitive to your surrounding environment. Make sure it meets your high standards. You would love a gorgeous, luxurious house, but this is not a necessity. What you do need is an orderly, clean, and comfortable space. It will help if you feel your surroundings are tasteful and attractive as well. Gracious and diplomatic, you have a flair for fashion and for hosting special events. Your marriage will thrive if you keep up with social outings, double dates, and family gatherings.

There's a core of strength in the Libra character. Although you may at times appear so, you're not wishy-washy. You can be shrewd, are usually very much in touch with how you want things done, and have the ability to get what you really want while keeping everyone around you happy. You've got an excellent sense of timing and will know exactly the right time to talk about moving, planning a vacation, or hiring household help. As you're a great negotiator—and polite and well mannered to boot—it's that much easier for your husband to give you what you want!

Libras operate on the pleasure principle. You don't like doing anything that doesn't please, stimulate, or relax you. Remember that in day-to-day life, there will be things that you must do that you don't particularly like. It's best to focus on working things out; your relationship will not grow if you continually practice avoidance techniques! And don't be unfair by continually allowing your partner to do the "dirty work." If your husband will swap duties with you or if he enjoys the things you dislike, that's fine. But in a home where everyone takes turns cleaning the bath, make sure you do so on your day. It's only fair.

It can be important to listen to what your husband is saying, rather than how he does so, especially if you have a moody guy. Many men have difficulty expressing themselves. While you may dislike the manner in which he occasionally sounds off, try to see what's behind the façade. Often you'll find your essentially cooperative, lovable man still there behind a cranky exterior.

Because Libras may avoid difficult situations, some could have a tendency to let a more assertive individual make decisions. It may feel easier to let your husband take over, but you'll be short-changing yourself in the process. If you really want to have a true partnership, you must make your own choices and take responsibility for them.

Perhaps the biggest problem for Libra people is indecisiveness. Many situations can force you to come to conclusions or to act quickly. While you know exactly what the perfect time for action feels like, it might be slow to arrive. Don't let yourself get hung up on the small things. For example, you may not know who to call first, so just make a call: any call. The world is full of ever-changing situations. You may have to call your real estate broker back after talking to the bank and reviewing things with your husband, but you may not have been able to avoid this in the first place.

# SHARING YOUR THOUGHTS WITH THEM

- **Aries:** You cool his jets; he fans your flames. Loving each other is learning how to adjust your thinking to the other's mental temperature.

- **Taurus:** You're diplomacy itself; he's tactful and polite. The relationship will ignite when you both say exactly what you mean.

- **Gemini:** You're both observant, with many ideas, sparking wonderful insights, and the ability to express them.

- **Cancer:** Your fair-mindedness is matched by his partiality. Trust his gut instincts; he'll learn to love your thoughtful meditations.

- **Leo:** You thrive on open discussion; he's more interested in his own ideas. Give an ear to his musings; he'll provide creative insight.

- **Virgo:** You treasure lyrical expressions; he's more concerned with telling it like it is. Find the common elements to strike a perfect balance.

- **Libra:** You both prefer feedback and time to weigh decisions. Don't get bogged down with the decision-making process—act!

- **Scorpio:** You each appreciate support and savor intimacy, sharing insights and secrets. But remember, there are others out there worth talking to!

- **Sagittarius:** You're cultured and refined; he's spontaneous and unrestrained. If you swallow his straight talk, he'll respect your decorum.

- **Capricorn:** You both select your words carefully. Take your time; this coupling favors solid, sensible compromise of even disparate views.

- **Aquarius:** You appreciate other outlooks, and he doesn't force his judgments on anyone. Together you'll treasure original insights.

- **Pisces:** You may both tiptoe around hot-button issues to keep the peace. A bit of direct discussion will deepen your bond.

# CHAPTER 8

# Scorpio
## (OCTOBER 23–NOVEMBER 21)

Scorpio people tend to be quiet and retiring by nature. Like the scorpion peeking out from behind a rock, you prefer a private atmosphere and will close doors, pull down blinds, and take other precautions to ensure that you're not easily disturbed. But you're very attentive to the outside world. Nothing misses your sharp, penetrating, and sensitive scrutiny.

Scorpios are committed to those they love and care for. You're loyal, giving, and emotionally supportive. Yet only a few people earn this caring treatment. The constellation Scorpio contains the bright-red star Antares at its center. We can see this as the passionate, intense heart of Scorpio. It'll glow brightly on your wedding day!

## WEDDING PLANNING

You Scorpios are realistic, resourceful, and independent. You often have a clear idea of what you want and how to go about getting it. Use these strengths to help you plan your dream wedding.

You may be too busy to do everything yourself, and many Scorpios prefer to delegate. A wedding consultant can take on any of the tasks you'd prefer not to handle. Many larger hotels will also serve as planners and handle everything from the rehearsal dinner to the ceremony, reception, and entertainment. This can save you a lot of time and aggravation. Just be aware that some charge top dollar for these services and could potentially be overpriced.

Whatever the level of direct involvement you take in your wedding planning, you can be a fabulous negotiator. Many vendors will trim their prices if you only ask. It's a rare Scorpio who can't get a better deal from florists, fabric salespeople, or finger-food vendors. A band will be cheaper with fewer players or if it plays for less time. Ask caterers about packages that include hors d'oeuvres or cake; they could be cheaper than ordering everything separately. You may get a quantity discount when buying favors.

You have a knack for legal affairs and finances, so don't overlook prenuptial agreements and changes needed to wills, insurance, and the like. These could bring up strong feelings but may be necessary. You easily work with credit but should carefully consider how much debt you're willing to take on.

Weddings are emotionally charged events involving many family members, and they can bring out the best and the worst in people. You might at times feel like you're on an emotional roller coaster. Be sure to carve out time to relax and take your mind off things that are aggravating you. Try not to build up annoyances in your mind. Don't exhaust yourself.

When you're tired, you may feel like you're trapped in a soap opera, wondering who's on your side and who's secretly getting annoyed. Don't take snafus personally. If you sense your perspective beginning to skew, consciously take a step back from the swirl of emotions. Call your most positive bridesmaid to brighten you up.

No matter who's paying for the wedding, you have a right to your preferences. But others, like your fiancé or your parents in particular, may have other priorities. If you've dreamed of a heart-shaped triple-decker cake trimmed in roses since you were a girl, insist upon it. For things that aren't as important to you, try to compromise. It may not come naturally to you, but giving in to your mom's demand to invite all your cousins may make everyone feel better. If you're stymied, fall back on your negotiating skills. You'll go to Hawaii on your honeymoon so your fiancé can surf, but he has to agree to take a volcano tour with you.

Don't keep your concerns bottled up. You're typically reserved and could stew for days or even weeks over an unfortunate comment or opinion. Talk things out with your fiancé or parents. Keep the connections with your bridesmaids strong; they can handle disagreeable duties for you and will also be there to listen when you need to let off steam.

And be sure to share your positive emotions as well! When your fiancé is stressed at the rehearsal dinner, take him aside and tell him how much you really care. Invest the time to think of some meaningful and memorable gifts for your bridesmaids and other members of the wedding party.

## STRESS-FREE!

Your emotional highs and lows will be more extreme during times of stress and pressure. Your strong feelings could lead to anger, followed by exhaustion. Moderate your feelings by sharing them with sensible loved ones who'll calm you down and help you be more objective.

Real activity, like karate, fencing, boxing, or weight lifting, should also help deflect negative energies into more positive outlets. Working with a trainer will keep you from pushing too hard or straining yourself. Or follow through on tasks that soothe and involve you—like gardening or furniture restoration. Acupuncture and massage can also help release pent-up energies.

Too much stress could lead to PMS, constipation, or hemorrhoids for Scorpios. Eating right; moderating meat; and getting plenty of fiber from fruits, vegetables, and whole-grain foods should help lessen these symptoms.

At your worst, you may be prone to addiction, so try not to overdo it with alcohol, recreational drugs, over-the-counter medications, or even prescriptions. More holistic remedies will heal your mind, body, and spirit—as can (you guessed it!) sex. So grab your guy and head for the bedroom when you're feeling out of sorts.

## LOOK GREAT!

You're the femme fatale of the zodiac, although you may often hide it beneath old jeans and a baggy top. But yours is a sign of transformation, so no matter what your usual style, you can create your dream look for your wedding day.

You've got the guts to make a strong dramatic statement. Let your imagination run wild to sensual fabrics like velvet or satin and anything flowing, glossy, or sheer. You'll go mad for beads, sequins, or crystals, so be sure to include some in your bodice, headpiece, or hair.

Most Scorpios love lingerie, so buy something extra special for this big event! It could tickle you to wear red or black, some of your favorites, underneath a light-colored gown.

Scorpios are often attracted to vintage clothing, and you can probably find a secondhand gown for less. Add your own personal touches, or treat yourself to a recycled designer creation that never goes out of style.

Your stylist can transform your usual 'do into many styles with the help of setting lotions, a curling iron, and pins. Scorpios love intricacy, so an updo with braids, twists, or knots suits you. Accentuate your Scorpio charisma by piling on the mascara and choosing vibrant hues for lipstick and nails. Dramatic jewelry, like a favorite necklace or a chunky ring, complete your picture.

## A PERFECT AFFAIR

You're essentially a private person, and you may prefer a smaller affair. Not attracted to the superficial or showy, you nonetheless strive to present a subtle sense of beauty and a restrained grace. You tend to embrace the timeless past, so you could be attracted to the traditions of your family, heritage, or religion.

Scorpios can be drawn to natural and perhaps somewhat mysterious settings: near hot springs or a water mill, or in a vineyard, cavern, or natural history museum. Your sophisticated side might prefer a classy restaurant, country club, bed-and-breakfast inn, or hotel.

Scorpios are often intrigued by the metaphysical and occult, and the most die-hard of you could choose a Wicca high priestess or spiritual counselor to officiate. You might like to have tarot or palm readings at the reception. A Halloween, rock 'n' roll, or mystery-themed party for your more creative spirit would be unique.

### Scorpio Flowers
Amaranth, calla lily, hibiscus, poppy, rose, geranium.

### Scorpio Gems and Stones

Black pearl, black onyx, malachite, obsidian, ruby, smoky quartz.

### Scorpio Colors

Dramatic tones of deep red and maroon; murky shades; dark crimson, violet, magenta, wine, burgundy, greenish blue, poison green, black, navy, taupe, brown.

## SCORPIO HONEYMOONS

You like exotic, out-of-the-way places, and you'd prefer to be alone with your new husband as much as possible. Escape on a houseboat or to a Caribbean island. Or indulge your sense of intrigue for volcanoes, the Amazon rainforest, Mayan ruins, or Egyptian pyramids with a tour to one of these outstanding locales.

### Scorpio Cities

Carson City, Nevada; Denver, Colorado; Helena, Montana; Honolulu, Hawaii; Lexington, Kentucky; Missoula, Montana; Palm Springs, California; Philadelphia, Pennsylvania; St. Paul, Minnesota; Tampa, Florida; Winston-Salem, North Carolina.

### Scorpio Countries

Antigua, Austria, Honduras, Hungary, Latvia, Poland, Turkey.

## LOVE AND SEX

Forceful but sensual and seductive, you're a woman to be reckoned with. A strong emotional bond is vital and can be one of your most significant passions.

You crave someone who's deep, intense, and incredibly loyal. Passionate men touch your inner core. Your natural sexuality is strong, and you also revel in the intimacy of a long-term relationship. You'll open yourself both physically and emotionally when you feel connected and committed.

Mysterious and dynamic, you exude sexuality and power. You have an intense need for sexuality and can be turned on by a battle for dominance with your partner. At times you're overwhelmed by your own desire. But it's not always about sex. Money can be a big turn-on, too—yours or your partner's.

You're attracted to slinky clothes, black lingerie, and secretly finding out all about your lover's past.

### Great Scorpio Dates

As long as you're alone with your guy, you won't care where you are! But you'll flip for sharing a corner table at an intimate restaurant or hanging in the den with some great music or thriller movies.

## SUCCEEDING AT LONG-TERM RELATIONSHIPS

Your emotions run deep, and you're looking forward to an intense, even consuming connection. Passion is an essential ingredient in all of your relationships, and it's all the more critical in your marriage. But you also like to act alone and often do your best without the assistance of others. You need to maintain a sense of self-sufficiency and independence within your relationship.

You do need some downtime from round-the-clock togetherness. An occasional solo spa weekend, meditation retreat, or evening alone absorbed in a movie will help you recharge your emotional batteries. You should also create a home environment that will provide you with at least some quiet and solitude. You would appreciate a cozy and comfortable room or corner in which you can be alone and undisturbed when necessary. Your husband will get used to your need to retreat—and may be well aware of it already.

You're by nature a very private person, and it's important for you to recognize the idea of joint property. Remember that even what you consider to be your personal desk is really part of your shared home. Your husband may look for tape or a paper clip there one day. So don't be upset at what you may view as an invasion of privacy! If you hold onto papers or other items that you'd rather keep to yourself, make sure that they're carefully locked away in a sturdy drawer or box.

You're naturally self-guided and self-sufficient, and take intense pride in all you do. You make your own decisions regardless of what others think and will not be intimidated or influenced by the opinions or ideas of others. Scorpios are realists by nature, but you'll often go by your instincts when making judgments; your instincts are frequently quite reliable. But you're now part of a team. Remember that your husband needs to have a say in things too. Don't get in the habit of overriding him! All good relationships need the give-and-take of both parties.

You'll be extremely patient in overcoming any obstacles and won't swerve from a committed path. You're quite loyal and protective of your loved ones. If you're having any difficulties in your relationship, be assured that you can work them out. Honesty will go a long way, as can consciously letting go of any past resentments and anger. Don't dwell on things that bother you, but try to work on them while focusing on those parts of your husband that nurture and support you.

Security is also important; you won't be happy on an uncertain financial footing. You have a great ability to face hard facts, are very much in control of your own actions, are disciplined, and plan well in advance. You thus easily achieve financial goals and also know how to use credit and insurance to your advantage. Planning your goals jointly with your husband will give you a sense of security, as you'll know you share financial stability. Whether it's a home purchase or starting a family, take the time to discuss, compromise, and finally agree on a plan.

You have a quiet strength and great personal magnetism when you're operating in a positive frame of mind. But you may not be conscious of how strongly you come across on a purely emotional level; this is one thing to try to become aware of. You're generally quite subjective and can benefit from trying to see your husband's point of view in order to understand where he's coming from. You'll benefit from seeing a broader picture by finding out what your partner thinks.

Always try to be tactful and avoid sarcasm. Some more direct signs just don't *get* it! Many signs, like Aries, Taurus, and Sagittarius, take things on face value. Try to understand his way of looking at things. This is very difficult to do, but when you begin to understand him better, it will go a long way in helping you cooperate. Tolerance of his shortcomings and recognition of his feelings can always help. Try to treat him as you'd like to be treated.

While you can be acutely aware of power plays, it's best to keep them as far away from your closest relationship as possible. And by the same token, if your husband has hurt your feelings, let him know. Silence or trying to give him his due will only hurt you and undermine your relationship, so avoid it at all costs. You know what your husband's character flaws and problems are. Work with him to improve them; don't lower yourself by punishing him.

When you keep your emotions in check, try to see things more objectively and use your determined and loving side effectively, you're sure to continue to thrive in a relationship that can't be beat!

# SHARING YOUR THOUGHTS WITH THEM

- **Aries:** His explosiveness lights your inner fire; he's fascinated by the way you contain your meltdowns. The passion of your thoughts keeps you connected.
- **Taurus:** Who's as strong-willed as you? He is! Don't force each other to change opinions, but try to see the world through your partner's eyes.
- **Gemini:** Your conclusions are firm; he's mercurial and changeable. Soak up his lightheartedness; he'll savor your subtlety.
- **Cancer:** You're both intuitive and perceptive, so you may feel you can read each other's minds. Exchanging spoken words will only fine-tune the connection!
- **Leo:** You can both be strong-minded and uncompromising. The disagreements may be challenging, but making up is delightful!
- **Virgo:** You're each known for precise expression and penetrating perception. Future planning and constructive discussions are a snap!
- **Libra:** You both may shy away from sharing your deepest raw thoughts. Addressing the real nitty-gritty will power this coupling.
- **Scorpio:** Though mutually intuitive, discerning, and deep feeling, you both tend to disconnect when hurt. Cool down first, then talk things out!
- **Sagittarius:** You both have a philosophical bent, constantly searching for answers. Discussing mysteries and metaphysics can put your own issues in perspective.
- **Capricorn:** Don't let your shared fears and insecurities compromise your intimacy! You'll easily understand each other when you speak up about your feelings.

- **Aquarius:** You're intensely focused; he's freethinking. For a meeting of the minds, you'll each need to modulate your stronger opinions!
- **Pisces:** You have a wonderful emotional and mental rapport! You'll get him to be more concise; he'll make you more imaginative.

**CHAPTER 9**

## (NOVEMBER 22–DECEMBER 21)

Up in the sky at night, Sagittarius the archer looks as if he's about to go galloping off to explore the entire Milky Way. You love freedom and independence and see these as values to be cherished. You need to move about and travel—your expansive nature always needs somewhere else to go! You naturally resent restraints or restrictions.

Sagittarius is the most genial and good-natured sign of the zodiac, with an optimistic outlook. There's an innate trust of others, natural honesty, and a direct and open nature. You love people and are eager to get to know them all! And you often can simply "luck into" great situations because you believe they can happen. Make your wedding one of these!

## WEDDING PLANNING

You're so enthusiastic you'll delight in all the fuss made over you and your marriage. Try to keep things casual and fun. This is one of the most joyful times of your life, and you should keep it that way! Surround yourself with friends and family members who are as upbeat and high-spirited as you are. Don't get bogged down by details. You can have your bridesmaids, caterer, and other suppliers handle all the petty minutiae for you. And consider hiring a wedding planner or banquet manager to handle all the boring chores that you don't even want to think about. You'll have more time to focus on the fun of this spectacular event.

If a relative or friend doesn't approve of your match or the way you're doing things, it just doesn't matter. Smile, move on with your plans, and keep your distance from negative influences. Nothing should spoil your special day.

Tell everyone you know that you're planning a wedding. Word of mouth goes a long way with Sagittarians! The more people you reach, the more recommendations and referrals of quality services you'll find.

Cultural and ethnic roots can be significant to Sagittarians, and you may want to include them as part of your wedding. Use these as a theme or as part of your food or dress choices, music, vows, or ceremony. You'll pay tribute to your family history, and your guests will be delighted to learn more about your heritage.

Your religious background may also be important and will guide you in the type of ceremony to choose. Many Sagittarians marry outside their own religion. You might choose to have both a priest and a rabbi officiate, for example, or simply have a judge or justice of the peace. But be sure to meet with any officiants beforehand; more traditional religions may not agree to share blessings at the same time. Some opt for two ceremonies—one religious and one civil. If you have a favorite clergyman, no matter what the affiliation, consider him or her. Writing your own vows and choosing significant poems or scripture to be read may more accurately communicate your feelings than a standard ceremony.

You'll want to plan a fabulous honeymoon—travel is what you live for, and the more exotic the locale, the better! There's nothing more romantic than a cruise or trip to a Caribbean island, a stay in an Italian villa, or a retreat to a Mexican beach. Or think about a destination wedding. These may actually be competitive in price and allow others to do much of the planning. But remember that you must plan early to secure airfare and hotel packages and to handle the appropriate paperwork. Start a search for packages on the Internet, or consult a trusted travel agent.

You love to do things big, but don't think beyond your means. You'd revel in a huge affair, along with a rose petal–strewn bed at the swankiest hotel in town and a private jet to zoom you away to paradise. Get real! Pamper yourself, but don't spoil your credit rating. Seek paradise in his arms, splurge on what you can afford, and compromise on the rest.

And don't forget to party! Be sure to plan a get-together for your bridesmaids well in advance of the wedding so that you can simply enjoy each other's company. The spirit and good vibes you generate will take you all the way through to the big day.

## STRESS-FREE!

You've got tons of energy and enthusiasm but may have a tendency to overdo things. You don't need to shop for a present for your groom, visit hotels for your guests, and book your honeymoon trip all in one weekend! Pace yourself. Take your time and do things bit by bit.

Stress can aggravate anxiety, asthma, or sciatica for Sagittarians. You may be prone to injury if you race around too much. You're likely to overdo it in many areas of life, so moderate your eating habits. It's so easy to grab that bag of greasy chips when you're crunched for time or stressed out. Opt instead for small portions of a variety of foods. If you still feel empty, have a big salad, a bowl of soup, or some air-popped popcorn.

You might become frustrated by the demands on your time or limits to your freedom while planning your wedding. Schedule time for jogging, Rollerblading, hiking, horseback riding, or other outdoor activities so you don't feel hemmed in. Playing with a pet or reading the comics boosts your spirits. Or text, call, or email a friend to vent.

## LOOK GREAT!

You'll want to dance 'til dawn, so be sure your dress lets you move. You may prefer a more casual gown or even a less-than-floor-length dress. Or consider two gowns—one more elaborate for the ceremony and a simpler, easier style for the reception.

Stretchy, sleek fabrics that won't get caught in the bathroom door are flattering and functional. You might fall in love with a multilayered style with a train but will feel hopelessly trapped in too much fabric before long. Low-heeled shoes are a must, and ballet flats are well suited to your active style. Don't forget that Sagittarius rules the derriere—you may want to accentuate yours with a bustle style or a big bow at the small of your back.

You look best in bright colors and may even want to break tradition and choose a colorful gown for yourself. Your ethnic background could provide you with inspiration, as many cultures have colorful wedding attire. If you're attached to white for yourself, go all out with your bridesmaids' dresses.

You'll love playful additions, like colorful jewelry, ribbons or bright accessories in your hair, and body glitter. More natural-looking makeup suits you, but you can afford bright nail polish and subtly colored eye shadow. And don't forget safety pins for that calamity waiting to happen!

## A PERFECT AFFAIR

You Sagittarians want to shout your love from the rooftops and are known for doing things up in a big way. Don't worry if the bridesmaids are adding up—there can never be too many for a Sag! You'd like to have as many guests as possible, with everyone on the dance floor and drinks continually flowing.

For your ceremony, due to the Sagittarian attraction to diversity, you might choose an interfaith ceremony, two clergy people, or a nondenominational minister. Inspirational speakers (including you, perhaps?) can enliven the proceedings. Be sure your maid of honor and best man are up for the task with great toasts! If not, grab some of your more voluble friends or family members and enlist them.

A destination wedding could well be your thing, but other Sagittarius settings include a zoo, baseball field, or refurbished barn. And many a Sagittarian has gotten the urge to just elope to Vegas! Don't worry—you can always have the party or a church ceremony later.

### Sagittarius Flowers
Blazing star, carnation, crocus, foxtail lily, gladiolus.

### Sagittarius Gems and Stones
Amethyst, blue sapphire, snowflake obsidian, sugilite, turquoise.

### Sagittarius Colors
Rich, full hues like royal blue, purple, dark blue, dark green, deep violet; blends of red and indigo; white, yellow.

# SAGITTARIUS HONEYMOONS

You want to go everywhere and do everything, but you especially love knowledge and adventure. Go to a Buddhist monastery, on a road trip, railroad tour, safari, or to a horse-riding resort. If it piques your zest for exploration, it'll make you happy.

## Sagittarius Cities

Atlanta, Georgia; Jackson, Mississippi; Kansas City, Kansas; Long Beach, California; Montgomery, Alabama; Pittsburgh, Pennsylvania; San Jose, California.

## Sagittarius Countries

Barbados, Dominican Republic, Estonia, Finland, Iceland, Kenya, Suriname, Sweden, United Kingdom.

# LOVE AND SEX

You're an adventurous free spirit who'll easily take risks for love. But you need freedom and won't be tied down. If you're taking the big step of getting married (and it is a big step for any Sagittarius!), he must be a special kind of guy.

Love for you is exploring your inner longings with each other. It's also about sharing your idealism and enjoying life to its fullest. Whether it's a 7 a.m. quickie or a leisurely weekend lovemaking session, you like to mix things up and appreciate variety.

Sex is a form of athletic activity, which your restless side craves. But when you also connect with your partner on a truly deep level, sexuality can even expand your consciousness. Profound discussions about the more philosophical questions of life and death thrill you.

Bright and inquisitive, you're turned on by anything that expands your horizons. You love adventure of all kinds—like an expedition into the South American rainforest or a safari in Africa. And perhaps you might also be a member of the "mile high" club!

### Great Sagittarius Dates

You'll enjoy Rollerblading, horseback riding, skeet shooting, or simply going for long drives. Sporting events, petting zoos, or action/adventure movies together are also high on your list.

## SUCCEEDING AT LONG-TERM RELATIONSHIPS

Bright and vivacious, you're always ready for a new adventure. In relationships, both you and your partner must feel free to explore the world and pursue your long-term goals. You might have a tendency to think too big at times and should try to be practical, especially about significant relationships.

Your positive attitude, need to share your thoughts, and jovial good spirits are a plus in marriage. You can easily enthuse your husband, inspire him when he's down, or keep the two of you laughing all night. Your perfect relationship is one with a man who'll discuss it all, whether it's religion and politics or just plain gossip.

You're idealistic and hold important beliefs. Often, Sagittarians are drawn to spiritual or church work or other public concerns that they believe in, and can be ardent political activists or cause crusaders. You'll make a terrific team if you share an interest or concern. If not, be sure you make space in your relationship to continue these activities on your own.

Many of you Sagittarians really do believe in truth, justice, and the American way, not to mention the goodness of God and all peoples.

Because of these traits, you have high moral standards and expect the same in your partner. You're adaptable to the needs of others and have a knack for making the best of any situation you happen to find yourself in. You laugh easily, enjoy life in general, and like having a good time.

You're blunt and direct and will blurt out just how you feel. But you should try to wait before you tell it all, as your mind is constantly changing! Your honesty, frankness, and candor are some of your most attractive attributes, but be aware of what you say to your husband. "You're getting fat" or "Your hair is thinning" are remarks that were probably said with openness and warmth, but he may be sensitive to his outward appearances, foibles, and shortcomings. Learn to become aware of his sensitivities, and save your sense of humor and high spirits for other topics.

You like to keep up with friends and can get a lot accomplished by telephone networking. In doing so, you're able to enjoy the stimulation of many people and places without leaving your living room. But no one likes to sit on the couch alone while his partner is off gabbing with everyone else she knows. Keep in touch with your friends and family, but don't allow phone or email time to intrude on your marriage.

You're generous to a fault and will offer any assistance to help others. But before you make promises, try to think in a practical way about what you can really accomplish. It may be fun to wash your car together or even clean out the garage. But don't offer to open a new CD at the bank or shred a pile of documents if you'll be crawling the walls after having to sit still for fifteen minutes.

You might also overestimate how much you can accomplish. It will take more than one weekend to paint the whole house or redesign your yard. Trying to squeeze things in will cause you to rush and leave you exhausted and short-tempered. Do both yourself and your husband a favor and don't overcommit to household tasks or outside activities. Be sure to leave plenty of free time for just the two of you.

Most important for any Sagittarian is the need to have a relationship that offers some kind of freedom. This can take the form of freedom to make decisions, ability to act independently, or latitude to do what you feel is best at any given moment, and could even include a physical sense of freedom through travel. Anything that breaks up routine is satisfying and welcome to you; you desire change, excitement, and variety. If you feel trapped and bottled up, you won't be happy.

Your need for movement and excitement may have led you to change relationships more frequently than most. Feeling controlled or tied down will push your "bolt" button. If your man shows any of these tendencies after marriage, it's best to have a long discussion about what you can't tolerate. You may also become more easily bored than most, so be sure to keep up with friends and activities that enthuse you. You have a yearning to explore the world, and travel or education with your spouse can help tame your sometimes restless spirit. If you can't afford to hop off to Hawaii or the Arctic every month, just taking a long drive or going for a spontaneous jaunt together should satisfy that restless spirit of yours.

## SHARING YOUR THOUGHTS WITH THEM

- **Aries:** You're both candid and spontaneous. The result? Lots of excitement—you'll never be bored!
- **Taurus:** You're two straightforward and clear-speaking people! Your lively conversation piques his interest; his steady outlook centers your thoughts.
- **Gemini:** The sparks can fly in this war of words, but behind the talk are two minds that enlighten and intoxicate each other.

- **Cancer:** You speak frankly, while he can be more coy. Learn to decipher his subtle messages; he'll enjoy your witty barbs.
- **Leo:** You're both upbeat, even outspoken. Impossible to say who's the better entertainer, so perform duets!
- **Virgo:** He's sensible; you're outrageous. Together you dream up, flesh out, and execute terrific ideas.
- **Libra:** You love the limelight; he speaks softly from the shade. Once you accept these minor differences, there's an open channel!
- **Scorpio:** You speak up; he defaults to reticence. But you two share an unforgettable passion that transcends talk.
- **Sagittarius:** Honest and frank to a fault, philosophical debates turn you both on. Your open minds draw you into each other's open arms.
- **Capricorn:** Your mouth runs free; he reins his in. Common ground: humor and irony. Add it to your ramblings, and you'll go far!
- **Aquarius:** You say, "I'll love you forever!" He says, "You're my best friend." The difference? Just semantics. Truth is, you're completely in accord.
- **Pisces:** Both poetic and visionary, you create your own private language and world to escape from the humdrum. Together, you're inspired.

# Capricorn

## (DECEMBER 22–JANUARY 19)

Capricorns have fine taste and discerning judgment. Did you realize that both angora and cashmere come from a goat, the symbol for Capricorn?

The goat is also known to be intelligent and playful and can even make a good pet. Goats typically eat almost anything, and Capricorns make good use of whatever resources they've got. You Capricorns have organized minds, think things through carefully, and often have a dry or cynical wit. While you know that marriage is a serious business, you need to find the fun in planning it too.

# WEDDING PLANNING

An organizer at heart, you'll easily plan ahead and are quietly committed to your future together. What works for you Capricorns is making a greater effort than anyone else. Your wedding planning could take up to a year or more. Use as much time as you can on a regular basis toward your planning.

Adopt a routine. This may include picking up a bridal magazine at the beginning of the month, doing research online in the evening, or visiting venues on weekends. Plan to spend at least some time every day or a set number of hours a week planning your wedding.

You're at your best when you can work in a slow and steady manner, so take your time. Faced with deadlines and commitments, anxiety can creep in. Do your best to start planning well in advance to allow time to explore all your options, study contracts, and assess prices. Decide how each of your relatives, friends, and bridesmaids will participate.

By building in extra days for delays and contingencies, you'll avoid anxiety. And don't neglect scheduling in time for relaxation—like an hour in a hot tub with your favorite music to clear your head!

Be prepared for the unexpected. When it turns out that the caterer can't supply prosciutto and melon at the last minute, it won't throw you if you've kept track of your second choice for an appetizer. And you may want to opt for wedding insurance. It's inexpensive and will reimburse you for anything from a lost gown to ruined photos to delay due to an illness or severe weather.

You tend to take things seriously, so make the effort to lighten up and enjoy this special time! You may be working so hard at getting things right that you overlook all the pleasures along the way. Make a date with your fiancé when shopping for rings. Savor the glamour of trying on gowns.

Appreciate the time you have to spend with your family and friends as you look for a hall or caterer.

You'll feel better when you're in charge and can take control. So don't just let a shower happen, for example. Let your maid of honor know what you'd prefer and who to invite. Be willing to pitch in if you want something extra special, or make it clear if you'd really prefer not to have a shower.

No matter who's paying for the actual wedding, it's important to be aware of boundaries. This may be the first family affair you're handling as an adult, so you need to stand your ground with those who have other ideas. Make your needs clear and don't get drawn into long discussions. Though your parents' wishes are always important to you, you probably have your own taste and preferences. Remember, it's your wedding, not theirs, no matter how much they may try to convince you otherwise!

The sign of Capricorn rules tradition and history. You'd probably be thrilled to get married in the same church as your parents or to wear a formal gown. But it's up to you which traditions to choose. If you want to write your own vows or have a more informal reception, it's completely up to you.

Capricorns can be torn between thriftiness and a desire for the best, so compromise. You might limit your menu and guests to save money, or consider a discount dress retailer. Your home could serve as an ideal location for the reception, with the savings allowing you to splurge on food.

Your honeymoon has probably been carefully arranged, but you may also want to pack in advance—or at least make a list of what to bring beforehand. It'll mean one less thing to think about as you get closer to the big day.

## STRESS-FREE!

You'll never miss a deadline—but you could exhaust yourself trying! You typically underestimate what you can accomplish, so learn to relax a little. Faced with the potential conflicts involved in any family affair, you may tend toward anxiety, pessimism, and even depression.

Organizing your time can help avoid stress. Get a good calendar or use your smartphone to keep track of all your to-do lists. And don't freak out if you don't check off every one tonight! Lots of things can wait until next week.

Continued stress could lead to dry skin, rashes, brittle nails, or even joint stiffness for Capricorns. Getting out in nature, hiking or mountain climbing, or getting together in a backyard or park with cheerful friends and relatives can also restore your spirits. Listen to your favorite music as you do some home aerobics, swim, stretch, or breathe deeply—anything that revives you.

Capricorn also rules the teeth. Take time out to brighten your smile with a whitener while you kick back with some classical music, an old movie, or a good book.

## LOOK GREAT!

Capricorns always prefer a classic, cultured look; you'd never go for shimmering purple eye shadow or yellow nail polish. Too gauche! A hint of lipstick and a touch of rouge are just fine by you. But as Capricorn rules the skin, you'll want to pay extra attention to your complexion. Visit a salon for a facial or indulge in a mud masque. Treat your skin more delicately in the weeks leading up to the wedding and stay out of the sun!

You should probably wear more makeup than you usually do for your wedding; invest in a good foundation or go to your favorite cosmetics counter for some advice and suggestions. Try a more elaborate hairstyle than your usual, but avoid it if it means the hairpins might be flying in an hour; you can't stand too much fuss.

You're a traditionalist who wants to look sleek but not flashy. Think appliqué and embroidery or a corset-style top. Many Capricorns love an old-fashioned, long-skirted ball gown with a jeweled bodice or long silky sleeves.

You prefer the sophisticated and simple in accessories, like a glittering gold or zirconia necklace, matching bracelet, and earrings. Or wear your favorite pearls, your mom's tennis bracelet, or your grandmother's perfume. You'll be prepared for anything with a credit card, your watch, and even a Swiss army knife in your bag!

## A PERFECT AFFAIR

Many Capricorns love tradition, and you can embrace it in various ways. You may be attracted to a picture-book ceremony with a well-known officiant in your family's church or synagogue. Bible verses or a favorite poem could be part of your ritual.

Capricorn settings include a rooftop garden, penthouse, estate, historic mansion, or mountain resort. Themes could draw on the past for inspiration. If you're attracted to a particular time, like the Victorian era or motifs from the 1920s or 1950s, use them! Consider a horse-drawn carriage to carry you to the ceremony or reception in style.

Take a little time to rehearse your first kiss as man and wife. Love for you is serious business. You may shy away from PDAs, so be sure your fiancé agrees on the level of enthusiasm involved in this very public act.

Do away with anything you feel is not classy—if you aren't comfortable taking off a garter belt in public, for instance, just don't do it.

### Capricorn Flowers
African violet, jasmine, pansy, philodendron, snowdrop, white foxglove.

### Capricorn Gems and Stones
Black spinel, black star sapphire, garnet, hematite, jet, sardonyx, smoky quartz.

### Capricorn Colors
Colors of nature and the earth; subdued colors; flat tones; black, dark brown, russet, beige, taupe, khaki, wheat, cream, gray, dark green, indigo, deep violet.

## CAPRICORN HONEYMOONS

You're sure to have planned your honeymoon well in advance and prefer more sedate and relaxed vacations. Try visiting a mountain resort, staying at a lighthouse or rustic lodge, going on a sleigh ride, or touring ancient places like Greek ruins or Machu Picchu in Peru.

### Capricorn Cities
Anaheim, California; Austin, Texas; Bethlehem, Pennsylvania; Cambridge, Massachusetts; Charlotte, North Carolina; Cincinnati, Ohio; Corpus Christi, Texas; Mobile, Alabama; New York, New York; St. Petersburg, Florida; Virginia Beach, Virginia.

### Capricorn Countries
Australia, Cameroon, the Czech Republic, Indonesia, Lebanon, Slovakia, Syria, Taiwan.

## LOVE AND SEX

Most Capricorns shy away from sex on a fire escape or in someone else's car. You prefer a quiet room, soft music, and comfortable surroundings. Even in private, you could still find it hard to show your feelings sometimes. If he says, "I love you," force yourself to respond—and not with "I know!"

You might benefit from a more spontaneous partner, and can afford to let yourself go in love. At times, the tensions of the day might make it tough to relax. If necessary, schedule in quality time to share with your husband. Unwind with a drink, some soft music, or just snuggling and chatting together. Focus on enjoying each other in bed, and don't let your mind drift to worrying about your supervisor's critiques or how to get your next promotion.

Once you feel secure in your affections, you'll have more abandon. A regular Friday night date or Sunday meal together can help you stay bonded. But don't be afraid to try something new from time to time. Having a passionate rendezvous in the morning rather than the evening, taking a special vacation, or exploring a new restaurant may be all it takes to spice things up.

### Great Capricorn Dates

You like calm, serene surroundings and would appreciate upscale restaurants, classical or oldies concerts, or lunch in a park or garden café. Or try a natural history museum or architectural tour.

## SUCCEEDING AT LONG-TERM RELATIONSHIPS

Only a solid commitment will do for you, and you'll work toward building a lasting relationship. You're extremely reliable, and you need constancy in your marriage. You have a deep sense of responsibility and a no-nonsense approach to life. A born executive, nothing is too much work for you, and you're more willing than most to work at your partnership.

You want to feel that your husband is as organized as you are—or at least that he doesn't interfere with your orderly outlook! Money is a concern to Capricorns. You're prudent and practical, so you should make it clear to your man that you intend to live within your means. You'll feel better when you know you have money in the bank and can save regularly. Your good sense coupled with a cautious outlook makes you someone who's well suited to handling finances. When in charge of funds, you'll be thrifty and resourceful and will save. You can make a little go a long way, like to plan purchases ahead of time, and can recognize a good investment when you see one.

It's important that you agree on finances. If your husband tends to run up credit cards or is cavalier about money, you need to compromise or even rein him in. Having a joint bank account but separate personal accounts may help. Or encourage him to use a debit, rather than a credit, card so he doesn't exceed your budget.

You're responsible and can be counted on to accomplish what you promise. Conscientious, reliable, and dependable, your husband knows he can rely on you at all times. You're usually committed to your family and will want to stay close with his too. Remember that you can't do everything. Try to keep up with family events. But if your marriage, work, and eventually your own kids are priorities, don't punish yourself with guilt and recriminations. Keep in touch with calls and emails if you can't make all the family events. Do the best you can. Learn when to say no to extra commitments or overtime at work. And you certainly don't need to wash the sheets or mop the floor every week! Give yourself a break and savor your time together.

All of you Capricorns can benefit from relaxing and enjoying life more. Remember that the word *caprice* comes from the same root as *Capricorn*. You would ordinarily rather attend to business than waste time. When you make the effort, however (and you should make the effort!), you can be witty, fun, and stimulating. Your husband will appreciate your continuing to socialize and lightening things up a bit from time to time.

Because you ordinarily project into the future, you may find yourself worrying today about tomorrow's challenges. It's not only debilitating, it's unproductive! Careful planning should eliminate your need for worry, but using mental discipline is the only way to alleviate it altogether. If you find yourself worrying about things that are out of your control, stop it! Concentrate fully on the tasks at hand or distract yourself in any way you know how. Chronic anxiety can be a habit; you can break that habit once you become aware of it.

You may have a tendency to be too cautious or pessimistic about making decisions and changes. As a rule, you don't like change, but in life it's often necessary and even beneficial. Buying a home or having children are big decisions that could be important to you. Don't put them off due to fear or worry. If you dwell on the negative, you'll get nowhere. Cultivate your talent for being a realist; try to see the good instead of instinctively seeing the bad. Look on the bright side and embrace the joyful things in life.

Attitude is everything. You'll do much better if you welcome each day in an optimistic, upbeat manner. Talk to people more. Your tendency to focus on work and obligations could eventually lead to loneliness and depression. Check these negative traits by sharing yourself and your feelings with your husband and consciously looking on the brighter side of things.

Finally, try to be more tolerant of your husband's opinions, instincts, and habits. If you take a look at the various husband profiles in this book, you'll see that most people are not as naturally conscientious or serious as you are. Really understanding that, as a given, can help you get along better with your spouse. Don't control him too much—and don't treat him like a child if he doesn't share your more mature perspective. Learn to appreciate his individuality.

You always plan well for the future, so building a relationship on love, trust, and shared goals will allow your connection to deepen as the years go by. You can say along with the poet, "Grow old along with me! The best is yet to be."

## SHARING YOUR THOUGHTS WITH THEM

- **Aries:** He provokes you to be more candid; you teach him some tact. Your dialects vary, but you both cut to the heart of the matter.
- **Taurus:** Both thoughtful, you'll thoroughly discuss your plans and take time to make decisions. Just don't deliberate the details for days!
- **Gemini:** Your mature outlook and his youthful one need adjustment to combine. Help him organize his thoughts; he'll share loads of information.
- **Cancer:** Many mutual interests—home, career, family—give you vast reserves of conversational fodder. Don't shy away from discussing profound passions!
- **Leo:** He longs to be king of the castle; you're a stubborn mountain goat. Both want the last word! Offer advice instead.
- **Virgo:** You each sound modest and unassuming but can be counted on to guide, support, and offer wise advice the other will easily adopt.

- **Libra:** You two are both aware of all the rules governing productive relations. Throw out the rulebook and share what you truly feel!
- **Scorpio:** Both reserved, the deepest feelings you share may stay tucked inside. They're easier to express not in words but in passionate deeds.
- **Sagittarius:** You're centered; he's all embracing. He helps you broaden your horizons; you'll help him see the trees despite the forest.
- **Capricorn:** Each real and down-to-earth, you'll both keep promises and say what's significant. Take time out for fun and games to brighten your perspective!
- **Aquarius:** Objective and practical, both of you prefer cool to sentimental. A powerfully thoughtful twosome!
- **Pisces:** Splendid synergy! Your feet are on the ground; his head is in the clouds. You complement each other's thoughts beautifully.

# CHAPTER 11

# Aquarius

## (JANUARY 20–FEBRUARY 18)

Aquarians hate limitations of any kind and excel in casting off old thoughts, ideas, and conventions. You feel change has a value in and of itself and are drawn to new concepts, the untraditional, and the eclectic. Yes, Aquarians can be rebels, but only because they like to move into the future and resent the restrictions of the past.

Your symbol is the water bearer, who shares the sustenance of life with everyone. Aquarians will democratically give freedom to others as well. You're tolerant of various beliefs, opinions, and goals. Part of the Aquarian principle is to agree to disagree—happily! Diversity just makes life more interesting, so most Aquarians enjoy long-term committed relationships.

## WEDDING PLANNING

You Aquarians always want to do something that's a little bit different or off the beaten path. You should begin by considering what unique and individual contributions you can make to your wedding. Aquarians often prefer things that are very special in some way.

Express your original streak. You're such an innovator and trendsetter that you'll have tons of fun experimenting with the theme, decor, music, or dresses. Part of the excitement of a celebration is sharing it with people who are close, so be sure to involve your bridesmaids in your brainstorming.

But don't go too wild. Sure, it would be fun to say your "I do's" while backpacking in the woods with your bridesmaids in distressed jeans and funky boots, but some traditions have their place. Try to dream up plans that will please you as well as everyone else involved.

There are many ways to inject originality while still maintaining a semblance of what people expect. You might choose not to have a maid of honor or even a bridal party. Attendants' dresses need not all be the same—a similar color can offer a nice change. And there's nothing written in stone that says you must wear white. If it looks bad on you, or you're just turned off by the nineteenth-century idea of purity, do something else. Wear a dress that makes you feel good, is appropriate to your theme or venue, or shows off a favorite color. And who says men shouldn't be invited to a shower? Here's another "rule" you can safely break.

Play it by the rulebook for the important things, though. If you're meeting with a clergyperson, for example, it might be inappropriate to share that while you don't really care about religion, it still gives you a good feeling to have everyone come together in church. Don't compromise; you couldn't possibly! But while lunching with your future in-laws to ask if they can help finance the wedding, think about dressing more conservatively than you ordinarily would—it might pay off. If you want to showcase your uniqueness, wait until after you've cleared these crucial hurdles.

In wedding planning, it does help to first narrow down your choices a bit. Don't allow yourself to become scattered by following up on a wide array of possibilities. A common fault is trying to pursue too many things at once or not committing fully to one. Something may stimulate you today but be forgotten tomorrow, so follow through on your ideas.

Most Aquarius people are likeable and sociable and usually know lots of people—you're one of the few brides who realizes that it's not just all about you! Contacts can be very important in finding a desirable venue or caterer. You're good at asking people for recommendations and may just know a jeweler's niece without realizing it. Remember the adage that with three phone calls you could contact anyone in the country, and use it to your advantage: it's true.

Special interest groups or organizations to which you belong can also be helpful in your planning, even if the group's purpose doesn't directly relate to your wedding. Many are there to serve their members in whatever way possible and will provide more contacts for you to use. The larger the organization, the wider your network can become; you might just find an eclectic florist in that friend of a friend within the group!

You're healthily assertive and won't accept being overcharged by vendors. Do some homework to find the going rate for videographers, dresses, and so on, and you'll succeed in closing the deal to everyone's satisfaction.

## STRESS-FREE!

You may be having so much fun planning your wedding that you don't even realize you're stressed out! But if you're having trouble sleeping, find yourself aimlessly surfing the Internet for hours at a time, or start feeling jumpy, face it—you're stressed!

An Aquarian's weak points are the legs and ankles. You may feel muscle spasms, cramps, or swollen ankles when you're tense. You can become nervous or high-strung, feel eyestrain, and your blood pressure could increase. Spending time with friends can always help, as long as you don't party 'til dawn! When you're pressed for time, you could turn to junk or fast foods, so try to avoid them. Opt instead for fresh foods whenever possible.

Most Aquarians are not the most athletic people in the world, but anything that gets your limbs moving, like modern dance, walking, biking, or a treadmill, should help you calm down. And be sure to schedule plenty of rest! If you can't sleep, try to relax with some good music, a movie, or a magazine. Escaping into a great sci-fi story or alternate-reality adventure could be distracting enough to settle you down.

## LOOK GREAT!

You enjoy experimenting with things like buzz cuts and tattoos, keeping one step ahead of everyone else when it comes to the fashion scene. You're tuned into funky, fun styles! Your looks can range from the latest trends, to bohemian, quirky outfits, to hip styles from the 1960s or 1970s. Signature trademarks like a line of ear studs will set you apart, or try high-heeled shoes, techno-jewelry, a bold belt, ear cuffs, or an ankle bracelet. Choose a look, be inventive, and make it your own.

A wedding dress need not be traditional or boring. You may prefer a pants outfit, a shorter skirt, or a hat instead of a veil. You enjoy light, airy materials that are sheer or fine and easily flow with your movements. Avoid anything that feels stiff or confining.

If you have short hair, style it with more volume than usual. Add lightness and movement, waves, curls, or a jolt of color—especially to longer hair.

One word of caution: be sure you look pulled together. As much as it may appeal to you, you won't look great in a short gown, paratrooper boots, and punk rock–style hair. Choose a special dress, hairstyle, or accessories to set you apart. Then plan the rest of your outfit to suit and enhance it.

You're connected to both mind and matter, so bring along your electronic organizer and hair gel for those stray locks.

## A PERFECT AFFAIR

Aquarian affairs can be contemporary, eclectic, and memorable. You're sure to put your own personal stamp on whatever you do and can come up with something creative, kitschy, and totally different.

*Casual* and *inclusive* are Aquarian bywords. Being the center of attention won't please you nearly as much as knowing that your family and friends all had a great time. A lunch or cake-and-coffee reception might feel more comfortable than a potentially stuffy sit-down affair.

It was probably an Aquarian who had the first bridesman or groomswoman at her wedding. You might prefer changing traditional language such as "Who gives this woman?" to "Who blesses this union?"

Intriguing Aquarian party locations include an observatory, a modern art gallery, or greenhouse, or you might choose to exchange vows in an airplane or a hot-air balloon. New Age–style themes like an outdoor moonlit celebration; feng shui–inspired affair with candles, chimes, and crystals; or even a science-fiction gala could all tickle your fancy.

### Aquarius Flowers
Arum lily, bird of paradise, coxcomb, sea holly, Thai orchid.

### Aquarius Gems and Stones
Aquamarine, chalcedony, fire opal, fluorite, lapis lazuli, sapphire, spectrolite.

### Aquarius Colors
Shocking shades; electric and glaring hues; psychedelic combos; bright blue, azure, violet, aqua, blue, green, yellow.

## AQUARIUS HONEYMOONS

You thrive on varied experiences and want to do something fun and offbeat. Think about going on an eco-tour with a group, staying at a nude beach, going for a helicopter ride, or taking a cruise to Alaska to catch sight of whales and moose.

### Aquarius Cities
Albuquerque, New Mexico; Ann Arbor, Michigan; Asheville, North Carolina; Birmingham, Alabama; Boulder, Colorado; Columbus, Ohio; Dallas, Texas; Hot Springs, Arkansas; New Orleans, Louisiana; Savannah, Georgia.

### Aquarius Countries
Grenada, India, Spain, Ukraine.

## LOVE AND SEX

You crave excitement and want a free-spirited and spontaneous romance. You're more attracted to a guy's mind than his body or emotions. Being part of a mushy, kissy, always-together twosome would make you gag. You like the feeling of friendship within romance.

Spontaneous and spunky, you love all types of relationships and have friends from all walks of life. You're an innovator who's never afraid to try something new. You're not shy about experimenting with sex toys or watching an erotic movie. Unconventional in your tastes, you delight in sexual exploration with your lover. You need variety and must keep the relationship somewhat unpredictable.

The intellectual could arouse you as much as the physical. Chatting in bed, talking about your friends and current events, and planning a social outing together can keep you intrigued and entertained. Phone sex, hot emails, and erotic poetry may all strike your fancy. Going to a dance club, funky bar, or bed-and-breakfast inn with him, especially if it's something new for you, could also spice things up.

### Great Aquarius Dates

You'll get a charge from sharing a sci-fi epic together, shooting a video, or going out with a group to the movies, a cyber café, or a planetarium.

## SUCCEEDING AT LONG-TERM RELATIONSHIPS

Aquarius is the sign of friendship, and you need a sense of camaraderie with your mate. You seek permanence but also freedom in relationships. This may sound contradictory, but you simply need to be sure to leave room for independence in your marriage. You'll feel stifled by someone who shows a possessive or jealous side. Your marriage will be strong if your husband encourages you to do your own thing; if you're too tied down, you'll feel like you're missing out.

An intellectual companionship is vital to you, especially if you can agree to disagree. You're not one to provoke quarrels or showdowns but would rather invite discussion. Sharing ideals, causes, or political passions with your husband can also help your connection stay strong. You'll be happy and content with someone who's mentally stimulating, intellectually challenging, or concerned with humanity as a whole. If you deeply love your husband but he offers none of the above, you need to keep up your own interests outside of home.

Variety and stimulation are necessary for Aquarians. There should be uniqueness to each of your days. While you can take mundane tasks for short periods of time, these should be varied with different things, places, and people. Get out with friends, go to a lecture, or explore an intriguing topic online. Whether or not you do these things with your husband, maintaining positive outlets like these will keep you from feeling restricted. Working as part of a group effort for the community or a special interest, or just having people surround you on a regular basis, will bring out the positive Aquarian tendencies in all of your relationships.

No matter how strongly you feel, discuss important decisions with your husband, especially financial and career decisions. Many Aquarians just don't understand money or position, and others may be more in tune with mundane realities than you are. And don't steamroll him into going along with what you want! You're used to going your own way, and it may take some effort to strike a compromise that suits you both.

While you're great at coming up with new ideas and suggestions, many Aquarians develop a habit of living in the future. You could get lost in the world of ideas to the exclusion of practical reality. Be sure you can afford that new bedroom set or kitchen remodel before you proceed. And don't surprise your husband with a major purchase, no matter how much you know he'd appreciate the gift. Plan it with him instead.

You don't ordinarily judge the actions of others, and you could potentially become too independent yourself. Remember to stay in touch and let him know where you are and what you're planning. A quick text message or phone call to check in can make all the difference between a worried spouse and a secure one. For you Aquarians, it's better to err on the side of caution.

While you'll ordinarily resent restrictions of any kind, most relationships have some of them. You dislike being tied down, especially to a specific schedule of household duties, and can benefit from varying your routine. If you're feeling frustrated, try a different approach toward duties and tasks. Sit in a different place to pay the bills, have a meeting or write a memo instead of making a phone call, talk finances over lunch, or simply explore new people and places together. You'll find all of these to be refreshing alternatives, and some can be implemented into almost any environment.

Because Aquarius is a mental air sign, you could have an alert and sensitive nervous system. Too many people, too many new ideas, or too many demands on your time can overexcite you. Make sure you rest and relax while at home; physical exercise can also help return you to your usual calm and collected state. Join forces with friends when possible. And a regular routine, as much as you dislike it at other times, can be a lifesaver during difficult periods. Knowing that you leave work at 4:30 p.m. no matter what and don't have to return 'til the next morning can help you clear your system. Don't try to do too much! Mental exhaustion could eventually lead to a depressed physical and emotional state. Your relationships will suffer as a result; use your good sense to avoid continued stress.

As you love the new, you'll be excited by the prospect of a new home or baby, a move, or other lifestyle changes. While a different routine and structure may take some getting used to, you'll soon be happily enjoying a new phase and sharing the next chapter of your life while married to your best friend.

## SHARING YOUR THOUGHTS WITH THEM

- **Aries:** You share curiosity and an attraction to new topics. You'll both find it easy to articulate your needs and desires.
- **Taurus:** You're rational and he's practical, but you each have your own way of looking at things. Don't butt heads; compromise!
- **Gemini:** You're both intellectually open and relish discussing the latest news and gossip. Sharing it will tighten your bond!
- **Cancer:** You communicate dispassionately; he's emotional. Accept his subjectivity, and he'll honor your fairness.
- **Leo:** Each strong-willed and committed to your own opinions, it's also evident that you're equally committed to sharing and candor.
- **Virgo:** You write in broad strokes; he dots all his i's and crosses every t. You easily adjust as you both share the ability to understand and analyze ideas.
- **Libra:** Two scintillating conversationalists! You have original observations, and he knows how to make it all sound wonderful.
- **Scorpio:** You're rational and thoughtful; he's emotional and passionate. Before you square off, consider what you really want from the exchange.

- **Sagittarius:** His sincerity warms you, and your freethinking thrills him. You can both be objective, seeing the big picture.
- **Capricorn:** You're attracted to new ways of thinking and he's drawn to tradition, but you both take the time and trouble to put what's important into words.
- **Aquarius:** You'll try to top each other with your unique and original interests. This combination is always provocative!
- **Pisces:** Both tolerant of the other's views, you understand the complexity of life. Find creative solutions by airing and sharing your concerns.

# CHAPTER 12

# Pisces

## (FEBRUARY 19–MARCH 20)

You Pisceans are warmhearted and giving people who need to help others and share your lives with them. But you also need periods or places of solitude so that you can recharge your emotional batteries from time to time. Still, you get along effortlessly with most people, are easygoing, and prefer to go with the flow.

Right-brained and otherworldly by nature, Pisces people are good at anything that stimulates the imagination and creativity. You need to bring out your dreams and visions to everyone else here on earth. A wedding is the perfect way to do it!

## WEDDING PLANNING

You're an idealist at heart who hopes for the best and thrills to the beauty, glamour, and romance of anyone's wedding—especially your own! You may have fantasies of the perfect wedding or many thoughts that don't quite fit together. Since your imagination can be of great help to you, take some time to dream up your ideal wedding. Then go one step further to describe your fantasy dress, ceremony, reception, and honeymoon. Clip pictures from magazines and brochures that appeal to you. Keep them all together and see what emerges. You should end up with some wonderful ideas that you can really use.

You Pisceans are great visualizers, so try to use this technique as well. As you relax or are falling asleep, visualize yourself at your wedding. See yourself as joyful and happy, surrounded by friends and family you love and care for. This should help you keep up a positive attitude and may also put out fortunate vibes on a subconscious level. A little unorthodox, maybe, but anything that can help in your wedding planning should be used!

Savor the present. This is one of the most exciting times of your life, and you'll want to cherish the memories forever. Take a day off from work and other chores to get your marriage license together, have a romantic lunch, and relish each other's company. Save pressed flowers, swatches from the bridesmaids' dresses, and your honeymoon tickets for wonderful wedding album additions.

Don't scrimp on photos or video, as these will give you some of your most lasting keepsakes. (You can save by requesting a basic package without special effects.) And you'll want to get plenty of candid shots from your photographer.

Mood can make all the difference, and you have the ability to create it with music. Pay special attention to choosing a band or DJ—will the music capture what you've imagined? Take some time to choose songs with special meaning, ones that evoke great memories, and those that will allow for dances with your dad, your new husband, and any others with whom you hold special connections.

It's important for Pisceans to keep looking, keep trying new sources, and to make a concerted effort in your wedding planning. Don't just drift along or while away your time Get out there and take action! Write down all of your appointments in a diary so you don't forget the whens and wheres. Punctuality is generally not a Pisces strength, so make an effort to be sure you leave in plenty of time to arrive early for a gown fitting or meeting with your banquet manager.

You Pisceans are usually not interested in finances, but money is an important concern. Don't ignore it. You may have a tendency to let expenses pile up—and they do add up quickly! Stay on top of your budget by keeping a list of what you've booked or spent so far. If you can't bear to face the tedium of appointments or financial concerns, put someone else in charge of them. Your maid of honor can keep track of your schedule, remind you of key dates, and even give you a wake-up call when you need it. Your fiancé or parents may be happy to keep track of the budget and expenses.

Keep yourself enthused and on-track by surrounding yourself with the beauty of your wedding. In dealing with all the details of planning, your fiancé may no longer seem romantic, and any disinterest in the wedding could disappoint you. Not to worry. Many men get "weddinged out." Assign him tasks that are second nature, those he enjoys, or is good at. Then go out for a nice meal and talk about all those other things that you usually enjoy doing together.

## STRESS-FREE!

You're so sensitive that you may feel daunted by the whole idea of putting together an entire affair. When your candles turn out to be the wrong color and your bridesmaids' gifts arrive late, you may just feel like running away! Don't worry, Pisces, you'll get through it all.

When you're stressed you may retain water, be more susceptible to colds or flu, and become sensitive to drugs or allergens. Your sign rules the feet, and they might bother you as well. If you're overworked or miserable, you may even develop nausea or fatigue. Listen to your body! Drinking could exacerbate some symptoms, so avoid too much alcohol.

Acupressure, foot reflexology, or almost any kind of gentle bodywork can soothe your spirits. Give your feet a long soak and let your fiancé massage them for you. Or get out and escape to the movies. You love the water, so head to a lake or beach for swimming, canoeing, or sailing; all could be restorative and help get your balance back.

Many Pisces people are artistic, and escaping from the outside world with a creative project, meditation, poetry, or music may be all it takes to get you smiling again.

## LOOK GREAT!

You have graciousness and charm, combined with an ethereal look. Create a storybook romantic fantasy with long flowing gauze and chiffon gowns and iridescent or sparkling accents in soft tones.

The femininity of lace, ruffles, silk, or fur always appeal to you. You might want to re-create a romantic vintage look. You can project true glamour once you have a clear image in your mind.

Show off your body. Look for advice and suggestions from fashion experts for accentuating your positive features. The style and proportions of what you wear can greatly affect your appearance.

Be extra certain to buy shoes that don't pinch and avoid ones with too high a heel, as your feet can be sensitive. You may prefer metallic sandals, weather permitting, or a fancy pair of ballet flats.

Soothe yourself with a pedicure or a long, hot bath before the big night, and slather on lotions and perfume to make you feel relaxed and sexy. Waves or soft ringlets in your hair might top off your look.

Complete your vision with pieces that strike your fancy, like a diaphanous scarf to drape over your shoulders, a sentimental ring, a lucky locket, or healing crystals. Whimsical or even humorous touches like feathers, jeweled hair combs, or a lacy garter belt are especially Piscean.

## A PERFECT AFFAIR

You'll want to create a magical fantasy for your special day, and a few significant touches will go a long way toward making you feel truly contented and fulfilled.

Your ceremony can be spiritual without being traditionally religious. You might choose religious vows and scriptural readings but could also include contemporary prayers, favorite poems, and candle lighting. Consider a moment of silence for relatives who may be gone.

Pisces places include watery locations like a sailboat or yacht, a beach, a grassy spot near a waterfall or lake, or even in the water! But you'll also enjoy the peaceful feeling of a favorite park or garden. Another important mood enhancer is music. Pisces can be attracted to a string quartet, folk singer, or a jazz combo. You might prefer a fancy cocktail and hors d'oeuvres reception for its light feeling.

### Pisces Flowers
Jonquil, lilac, lotus, Madonna lily, narcissus, orchid, violet.

### Pisces Gems and Stones
Alexandrite, amethyst, aquamarine, blue lace agate, coral, light green emerald, water opal.

### Pisces Colors
Etheric colors; pastels and watercolors; shimmering tones; diffused blues; sea-foam green, aquamarine, teal, heliotrope, violet, lavender, mauve.

## PISCES HONEYMOONS

Soothing and artsy vacations where you can do whatever strikes your fancy at the moment are best for you Pisceans. You'd also love a sleepy, romantic retreat. And of course vacations near water, where you can go diving, sailing, swimming, scuba diving, or communing with dolphins may be at the top of your list.

### Pisces Cities
Abilene, Texas; Atlantic City, New Jersey; Bangor, Maine; Ft. Lauderdale, Florida; Greensboro, North Carolina; Norfolk, Virginia; Provo, Utah; Roswell, New Mexico; St. Louis, Missouri; Tallahassee, Florida; Washington, DC.

### Pisces Countries
Ghana, Mauritius, Mongolia, Nepal, St. Lucia.

## LOVE AND SEX

Sweet and sensitive, you give your heart totally to your love. You'll swoon over sentimental love notes, poetry, or flowers. You love intimate dinners with wine and candles. Champagne, cocktails, slow dancing, or taking a bubble bath with your husband surrounded by soft music can put you in a sexy mood. You have what it takes to create magical, romantic nights.

At times you may be content to dream about what you want, and you can appreciate a platonic or spiritual relationship. Once you're involved in intimacy, however, you get swept away by the glamour of romance and forget everything else. Sex for you is a blending of two souls, not just two bodies. Taking time to relax in quiet, peaceful surroundings or sharing happy memories makes you feel more connected. Play with your cat together, listen to the soundtrack of a great Broadway musical, or just plan an incredible vacation. It doesn't really matter whether you ever get there—sharing the glow is what it's all about.

### Great Pisces Dates

Simple things like watching the sunset or the stars come out will touch your soul. Sharing a boat ride or a shady bench in a quiet park will warm your heart.

## SUCCEEDING AT LONG-TERM RELATIONSHIPS

Understanding, sympathetic, and compassionate, you get along easily with others. Your modest, unassuming personality makes you a good listener. You have an easy manner and are comfortable to be with. Your gentle, kind ways make you a nice person to have around, and your good sense of humor helps lighten up heavy discussions and keeps your marriage light and fresh.

You're able to adapt yourself to the demands of partnerships and aren't usually upset by changing circumstances. If your marriage demands certain restrictions (he works at night or on the weekends, for example), you'll handle them rather easily.

You need a little pampering: flowers every now and then, a foot massage, or sharing a glass of wine together. You profoundly appreciate it when your mate indulges your fancies, tolerates your quirks, and soothes you when you're shaken up. What if your guy is not naturally the most romantic person in the world? Turn him into one by going out for exotic restaurant meals, slipping away for a weekend at a country cottage, or dressing up in your slinkiest lingerie.

As most Pisces people enjoy at least some time alone, you'll find it refreshing to sit quietly for a period, peacefully listening to a CD, enjoying a natural setting, or taking a scented bath. It's important to make room in your life for contemplative time. If you can do this with your partner, so much the better! You're very sensitive and might be disturbed by the emotional excesses of those about you. Try to avoid disturbances by regularly tuning them out and focusing on things that bring you peace.

You like to give of yourself, and your natural instinct is to help out. But don't let this tendency undermine the balance in your relationship. You can tire or even exhaust yourself by trying to do too much for your husband. Learning how to say no is a difficult lesson for Pisces people, yet it can be essential toward maintaining a cooperative and healthy relationship.

Your self-effacing personality will keep you outside of direct confrontations, conflicts, and power struggles. You're just not interested in these things. You're great at avoiding disagreements, but at times you may not even be in touch with what you feel. Try to tune in to your own moods and feelings, and keep the lines of communication open with your husband. If he's sensitive and empathetic, he could even help you better understand yourself and your inclinations.

All Pisceans can benefit from assertiveness training! It's too often the case that a good Pisces mate will let her spouse take over in some way. Stand up for yourself, especially if you feel strongly about a course of action or are uncomfortable with a joint decision, even if you don't exactly know why.

Your ability to sympathize and see the viewpoints of others can cause you to be easily influenced. Learn to trust your own intuition in decision-making. If you doubt yourself, find some time alone to clear your mind; you'll find you make the best decisions in times of repose and relaxation.

Most Pisceans crave variety. You might become bored with a routine, a situation, or even a person! It's fun to flirt or fantasize, but you want your marriage to last. Don't allow yourself to drift into outside entanglements out of restlessness or boredom. Enhance every day by being sure to share something you both love. Vary your schedule and activities and go out with friends. Returning to the love of your life after being out will help you deepen your connection while keeping you fresh and stimulated by other people and things.

You can be kind and supportive and will dedicate yourself to your partner. When you've found that perfect person, it can feel like a spiritual connection that was destined to happen. But avoid deceiving yourself with idealism, as it could lead to disappointment. You can be attracted to men who need you to reach out and help them. Make an effort to see your husband's flaws for exactly what they are, no more or less, and gently guide him to improve. If you have a difficult partner or are emotionally uneasy in your life together, you won't do well. What's more, you won't feel well, either. Make a real effort to identify exactly what's bothering you and address the issues.

You might abruptly decide to call it quits if the mood strikes. Realize that this may be just a passing fancy. Discuss your feelings with some trusted, objective friends, and confirm your instincts when you're more relaxed. Perhaps speaking with a therapist could put things in a clearer light. You may simply be feeling disappointed, isolated, or lonely, and all of these things can be worked out if you make the effort. No Pisces should ever give up on love!

# SHARING YOUR THOUGHTS WITH THEM

- **Aries:** He puts things right out front; you may beat around the bush. But you share an intensity of feeling that helps bridge the gap.
- **Taurus:** You both prefer soft, unspoken signs of affection. Exchanging a few words now and then won't rock the boat!
- **Gemini:** You speak the language of poets and wizards; he's into nuts and bolts. You intrigue his mind; he stimulates yours.
- **Cancer:** He's visionary; you're creative. Together you'll dissolve ordinary boundaries and solve practical problems with imagination.
- **Leo:** You both feel strongly, with open hearts. But each needs to be less emotional when discussing issues you care about.
- **Virgo:** Your deep need to help and support each other drives you to ask, intuit, and analyze 'til you understand what the other truly needs.
- **Libra:** Your mutual responsiveness could lead to "I don't know. What do you want to do?" One of you non-egos needs to take a stand!
- **Scorpio:** Your stability lies in accepting all points of view; he gains from strong opinions. You understand each other so well it's never an issue.
- **Sagittarius:** You both appreciate new ways of thinking, seeing, and feeling. You'll introduce each other to new means of expression—and new cultural vistas.
- **Capricorn:** You're an optimist, he's a realist. Between your rose-colored glasses and his cloudless ones, you'll happily see what's really there.
- **Aquarius:** You share active imaginations that allow you to get into other people's heads. But don't assume you can always read your partner's mind!
- **Pisces:** You both need to be comfortable and relaxed to express best. Take time to unwind before important dialogues.

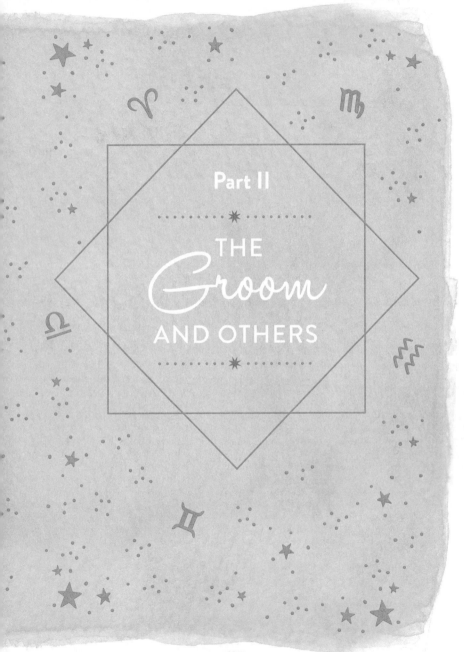

**Part II**

---- ✳ ----

THE

*Groom*

AND OTHERS

---- ✳ ----

# CHAPTER 13

# Aries

## (MARCH 21–APRIL 19)

This confident, vital man has a take-charge attitude and energy to spare. If you're active and outgoing, great! But don't expect him to sit and watch *Antiques Roadshow* with you all the time. He's better at helping share home-repair projects or shopping for a new car. Dynamic and popular, he's a natural leader. A vigorous macho type, you might find him on a baseball or football team or out in the yard fixing the lawn mower.

## YOUR ARIES HUSBAND

You already know he's got terrific vitality and the most upbeat attitude of anyone you know. Will he still be the same after a year of marriage? Yes! Aries men are always up for something spontaneous. It makes keeping the new, fresh, just-fell-in-love feeling easy. Want to surprise him with a weekend out of town? He's game! A night at a hotel just for the fun of it? He'll be there! Just be sure you keep track of how the spending is adding up, as he might not.

Aries men are open, honest, and straightforward. If your husband really hates the new dress you just bought for your first anniversary, he'll say so. And if he says it a little too bluntly, don't take it personally. Aries men speak their minds and don't really understand how to be tactful if it means being less than candid.

Aries men are engaging, friendly folks who enjoy others. It's a good bet that if there were a vote for most popular sign, Aries would win. Your Aries man craves companionship, but if you need time to yourself, he'll happily go out with friends, so you won't ever feel stifled. People born under this sign are so energetic and high-spirited that they infuse all activities with excitement and appeal. "Who wouldn't want to be an Aries?" they imply, as they get 101 tasks accomplished in a seemingly effortless manner.

You'll succeed in your relationship with your husband if you can remember one rule about Aries: what you see is what you get. An Aries is blunt and straightforward. His tongue is apparently linked directly to the brain—as soon as he has a thought, you'll hear it! Don't look for hidden meaning, covert implications, or subtext in his conversation. It's not there. You may hear someone referring to your Aries, saying, "What do you think he meant by that?" The answer is always crystal clear—just what he said, no more, no less.

Aries men can amuse and stimulate others with their frank manner but might cause some hurt feelings along the way. They feel so comfortable and at ease with others and are so absolutely unselfconscious about themselves that they'll really just say anything. They don't have a clue about how they come off to others. More sensitive signs like Cancer, Scorpio, and Pisces will be thrown by what they consider to be the sometimes tactless behavior or even obnoxious attitude of the Aries husband. No matter what sign you are, realize that Aries is an open book. Yes, an Aries can be too outspoken at times, but you can count on him to be completely honest about his feelings and desires.

Impulsive and spontaneous, the Aries husband loves to be surprised with your sexual overtures at unexpected times and places. Adrenaline is his aphrodisiac; hiking, cycling, and rock-climbing can get his erotic juices flowing. You'll probably be thrilled to travel with him. His enthusiasm makes him an extremely likeable companion, and any Aries will dig in with all the excitement nature allows.

Aries men are decisive and action oriented. They like to be on the go and can get a lot accomplished. When delayed or thwarted, they easily get excited. If you raise your voice with an Aries, expect him to instantly respond in kind. These are impulsive, impatient people who quickly let off steam. They can be hot-tempered and love a good argument. Your husband will fight first and ask questions later. If you don't mind a heated scene to clear the air, go for it! Once his anger is out, he usually cools down fast.

You may hear one too many unkind words about yourself. The remedy? Forget about it. Ariens don't hold grudges and are too busy doing what they're doing to remember they were mad at you. And they genuinely like people and accept them as they are. They just have ten times more adrenaline flowing through their veins than most of us and generally forgive and forget. Remember, too, that apologies are not your husband's style. Raising his voice is no big deal to him. If pressed, you'll probably hear "You drove me to it!" and the argument will begin anew. Accept as your apology the fact that on next contact, your guy will be just as charming and loving toward you as before. And remember that the Aries bark is often worse than his bite.

Aries husbands usually see lengthy discussions as a big waste of time. If you're stubborn enough about your point of view, you'll win out in the long run—an Aries frustrated by lack of action will eventually compromise just to get it over with!

Aries will quickly take the lead to make decisions and expect you to follow through. If you can handle this, you'll make an excellent team. If you can't, you'll have some frustrations. Cancer, Libra, and Capricorn wives especially may have problems with the Aries insensitivity and inability to come to mutual decisions. You'll also find that Ariens have a hard time planning ahead. They want to get things done now and move on to the next project, becoming distracted by the anticipation of any new activity.

In dividing tasks, remember that Aries men love to deal with people. Errands outside the home, telephone calls, and talking with people in the neighborhood will all stimulate him. Excess paperwork, delay, and discussion over details will frustrate and squelch his fiery tendencies.

In most situations, you'll find Aries to be companionable, hardworking, and honest. If you don't mind the excitement of a high temperament and can overlook some blunt remarks, you'll have a trusted and passionate partner.

### Positives

Aries men are straightforward and uncomplicated. They're lively, energetic, and fun to be with.

### Negatives

He's so into himself he'll expect you to follow along. And he never sits still, which could get tiring! He can say, "I love you" in the heat of the moment, then go off to clean the gutters.

## YOUR ARIES IN-LAWS

The Aries in-law is youthful, fresh, and spontaneous. He or she is a lively, fun individual who's interested in others and loves to talk. Shy about your first lunch alone with your Aries mother-in-law? Ask her a question about her son, and she'll talk for twenty minutes while you enjoy your meal! Aries men are likewise gregarious, and your Aries father-in-law will be happy to share his anecdotes about his son's first driving lesson or earliest girlfriends.

These are active, energetic people who may hold down full-time jobs while pursuing varied social lives and taking good care of their homes and families. They get much accomplished and will gladly help you with household projects or take you to the mall to hunt up a gift for your husband's birthday.

Aries in-laws are self-confident and feel good about themselves. They can be bold and outspoken, though, so if you don't really want criticism, don't ask them what they think of your new kitchen. They may offer it anyway, so brace yourself. Yet these people are generally too involved in their own activities to interfere too much in your life. Enjoy a ski weekend with them, let them babysit your kids, or invite them to help you prepare a Thanksgiving dinner. You're sure to appreciate and enjoy their company.

## YOUR ARIES MAID OF HONOR

Are you the sensitive type? Do you gravitate toward a calm and relaxed atmosphere? Do you need someone to follow orders? Then this is not the attendant for you!

Aries are leaders par excellence. They're completely comfortable when in charge and will expect others to be as quick, active, and optimistic as they are. If you're a laid-back type who needs to take lots of time and are working with an Aries maid of honor, you're in for a challenge. She may not have the patience to leaf through books of invitations, consider a variety of party decorations, or try on a dozen dresses with you—she'll want to quickly come to a decision and may accept the first best thing that comes along.

An Aries likes to feel she's in command; she wants to be looked up to and recognized as the one in charge. Ariens are easy people to get along with and are usually likeable, but they can be demanding. They'll address their responsibilities as if there were deadlines looming imminently. Strangely enough, however, in real crises they keep their cool and get no more excited than usual. A challenge is Aries heaven.

In general, these people are independent and expect others to be. If your maid of honor sees that the bridesmaids are going for their fittings in an efficient manner, she won't hassle them. An Aries likes to have others worry about the follow-through.

You may find that your maid of honor cannot anticipate deadlines; she may be so tied up in this week's problems that next week's priority seems minor in comparison. You'll have to keep her focused forward and do your best to prepare.

Don't be afraid of being assertive with this attendant. An Aries is very straightforward and relates to you best when you're that way too. If you want her to help you screen musicians or find a videographer, don't expect her to pick up on hints. Asking for what you want is the best way to find out what your maid of honor will do for you. She'll be great at scouting for reception sites or checking out hotels—anything that keeps her moving and gets her out and about.

Take seriously whatever this maid of honor suggests—she knows efficiency. If you can meet the demands of working with this active woman, your wedding will be pulled together in no time.

# CHAPTER 14

# Taurus

## (APRIL 20–MAY 20)

Taurus men take their time with anything they do. Mellow, steady, and deliciously laid back, Taureans are relaxing to be with. Ruled by Venus, the planet of love, Taurus men are typically steady and loyal. They know how to enjoy life, have well-padded savings accounts, and warm homes— all great for creating secure family environments.

## YOUR TAURUS HUSBAND

One of the things you'll treasure about the Taurus husband is his consistency. He doesn't just love you today, he'll love you tomorrow, and the next day, and the next. You'll always have the feeling that he'll be there for you, whether he actually tells you about it or not. Taurus men are not big on talk. What they are big on is action—your husband will show you he only has eyes for you.

Taurus men are more domesticated than most. They love their homes, are usually good earners, and can be counted on to join you in planning your dream house or family. Your Taurus husband will enjoy going out to eat or helping you prepare a three-course gourmet meal. He's romantic, warm, and cuddly—the perfect guy to share a fireside and some hot cocoa on a rainy night.

But he *is* stubborn, as you probably already know, and some of his bachelor habits may take time to break. Have patience! Once he finally gets used to doing the dishes or putting the toilet seat back down, he'll be trained for life.

Taureans seek peaceful existences and are usually kind, warm, and gentle. You can tell a lot about them by the way they speak: quietly and calmly with well-modulated, often beautiful voices. They prefer a relaxed, quiet environment and tend toward good-natured reserve.

Taureans go about everything they do in the same unhurried, unruffled manner. They crave material security and most will eventually own property or have extra money in the bank for a rainy day. These people like things to stay the same. Some may even wear the same suit constantly or keep it for ten years. Your Taurus husband might be an absolutely immovable, permanent fixture in front of the TV in the evening and will leave at the same time every morning, having eaten the same breakfast and read the same newspaper. Part of the reason he maintains such a placid disposition is that his inner sense of security is grounded in a lot of permanence and stability.

The good thing about living with a Taurus is that you'll always know what to expect. He'll react predictably and tend toward accepting the status quo rather than making any attempt to change things. He'll be extremely straightforward, up-front, and genuine; what you see is what you get. Literally. When he says he'll do something, he'll usually do it, although he'll take his time. If you confide in him, he'll never tell. Once he loves you, it's a final decision.

There's a great quiet strength in these earthy people, and they let a lot of pressure slide right off their backs. Taureans won't be rushed or hurried and won't allow themselves to be pressured into quick decisions. This is one of the most stubborn and obstinate of all signs once a decision or conclusion has been reached.

The peace-loving bull doesn't ruffle easily. Provoking him to anger will only bring out his stubborn and defiant side. Instead, take time and patience to get him to take out the garbage...and remind him, remind him, remind him!

When your Taurus has had enough, all the neighbors will know it. He'll explode into such a rage that you may be shocked. Remember that it does take a lot to provoke such a peaceful person to a state of violent emotions. If it's enough to rock the typical Taurean placidity, it's enough to cause a loss of control. Be forewarned. If you sense resistance, don't push this guy too far.

Taurus is a sensual sign. Warm and indulgent, the Taurus man enjoys foreplay as much as sex. Don't rush! He loves to be stroked and petted, so massage his back with a softly scented oil to relax him. These people love food and drink and consider a fine meal one of the chief luxuries of earthly existence. Over a rich dinner, your Taurus will become more relaxed and may even become a bit more expansive and talkative. Just be aware that many of this sign are often dieting as a result of being too indulgent!

Remember that your Taurus man can be extremely opinionated. Once he latches onto an idea, it may be nearly impossible to dissuade him from it. Get set for a long, detailed convincing session, complete with extensive cross-examination if you disagree. Taurus discussions can make even the most patient wives lose their cool, so be prepared for the long haul when dealing with this stubborn man. Even after you feel you've made all your points clearly and convincingly, you'll still find that your husband has to take more time to chew things over and think about them alone before making a decision. But once he's learned something from experience, he won't ever forget the lesson.

Avoid losing your temper, which many of you may be pushed to do; the sometimes incomprehensible Taurus stubbornness can be provoking. If your husband senses blind opposition or anger, he'll dig in his heels and become even more committed than before. It's a curious thing, but the more others oppose Taureans, the more determined they become to prove themselves right.

Be reasonable, practical, and patient with your Taurean when working out problems. He'll respond to kindness as well. You may even be able to appeal to his soft emotions. Taureans are known to bend when those they care about plead a case emotionally.

These men can be almost childlike in the black-and-white, good-or-bad way in which they view the world. They can also be somewhat naive compared to other more worldly, complex personalities. If you have unwillingly upset or hurt your new husband, just apologize and explain. The more stubborn and inflexible Taurean can hold a grudge. He won't be aggressive, mean, or overtly antagonistic, but he can make you uncomfortable nevertheless.

For the most part, however, Taureans are sweet, gentle, and reliable. If you can consistently show him love, concern, and friendship, you'll be sure to have a loyal, trusted partner for many years to come.

### Positives

This man needs someone to hold onto! He wants your relationship to last and is sensible, realistic, and down-to-earth.

### Negatives

He can be stubborn. Once he's made up his mind, he probably won't change it. And he's not the greatest conversationalist in the world. He could be possessive and jealous if he feels insecure about you.

## YOUR TAURUS IN-LAWS

Taurus in-laws are solid citizens. They usually have beautiful homes filled with comfy sofas and surrounded by gracious gardens. You'll admire your Taurus mother-in-law's fine china, linen, and jewelry. The Taurus father-in-law is probably a casual dresser and may have put on a few pounds. But both will probably have secure jobs that they've held for years.

These are relaxed, stable people who don't like to have their feathers ruffled or do anything quickly. Invite them over for a home-cooked meal rather than out to a basketball game. Or take them to the theater or a classical concert instead of the stock car races. They'll be perfectly content to watch a movie with your kids on a Saturday afternoon.

Taureans instinctively know about money and finances and can help you manage your checkbook, understand financial statements, and invest wisely. Your mother-in-law will know quality in a dress, furniture, and housewares, so she's a good candidate to take shopping—as long as you don't want to rush through all the aisles!

Taurean in-laws may be stubborn and inflexible at times and will often resist changing their ideas and opinions, no matter how much you disagree. But their emotional commitment is unconditional. Savor the Taurus warmth and soothing spirit when you need it!

## YOUR TAURUS MAID OF HONOR

Taurus maids of honor are particularly gifted in one area: they have an innate and complete understanding of the value of things. This can mean that they've got artistic taste, financial vision, or great practicality—maybe all three. Taureans are realistic; they know what's possible. Their common sense and no-nonsense approach can help you evaluate a caterer, bargain with a florist, or judge what gown looks best on you. Your maid of honor will take time to go through the bridal registry thoroughly and carefully.

Taureans are naturally patient and always take their time over even the simplest matters. You may have to wait for your maid of honor to plan the bridal shower or help choose invitations. Get used to it and learn to prod her regularly! It can help to have a meeting or phone call every week to review what's going on and keep her on schedule.

Your maid of honor will not be easy to oppose, convince, or sidetrack, however. If you get stubborn resistance to your choice for the bridesmaids' dresses, see if you can compromise. A Taurus can literally be immovable, sitting with her arms crossed in the dressing room, waiting for you to change your mind. You'll save yourself a lot of aggravation, time, and trouble if you learn that your maid of honor is a strong-willed person.

A Taurus is usually easygoing, though, and will overlook a lot of problems. She won't overreact if you call her hysterically one night to suggest that the wedding is off, and she can be counted on to calm and soothe your ruffled feathers.

As Taureans know the value of things so well, they also think they know the value of people. Sometimes they can have prejudices. Even if you feel the best man is the loveliest person in the world, your maid of honor may disagree. If she persists, make it clear that the decision's been made. Then just drop the subject and don't let her bring it up again.

It's very easy to get along with a Taurus maid of honor on a superficial level and more difficult in a close working relationship. But if you're willing to listen to her thoughts, roll with the flow, and assert yourself when she disagrees, you'll have no problem collaborating with this woman. And you'll have as your reward a stable, secure friendship that you'll continue to enjoy long after the wedding is over.

# CHAPTER 15

# Gemini

## (MAY 21–JUNE 20)

Intelligent and quick-witted, Gemini men have a gift for gab. Like a fine champagne, your Gemini husband will make you giddy with his wit, charisma, and easygoing ways. Thoroughly adaptable, he'll as happily attend a formal affair as take your nephew to a ball game. Overlook the fact that your girlfriends all find him charismatic—he's coming home with you.

## YOUR GEMINI HUSBAND

Bigamy is illegal, but the authorities won't know that you've got two men in one! Gemini is the sign of the twins. You'll find that your Gemini husband is so brilliant, flexible, and versatile that you might just end up wondering how many men are really inside that body.

This guy is youthful and refreshing, no matter what his age. Geminis have a vivacity and restlessness typical of the young. With an insatiable curiosity, they give the impression of being here, there, and everywhere. They don't like to be tied down to routine and are often in motion.

Your husband needs to keep his mind stimulated by talking to lots of people and learning about new topics. You'll find he has a lively interest in keeping up with friends, news, even gossip. He'll love spending an evening with other couples. Keep him in line by bringing him home before the wee hours, as he can get overstimulated with too much of a good thing.

Social butterflies, Geminis need to have people around them to be happy, and in turn will enlighten, entertain, and fascinate others. Geminis are at once familiar, casual, and bright. They speak with charm, ease, and fluency; can provide a near-constant stream of news and information; and have a light, impressionable way of communicating. Many Geminis also have infectious senses of humor. They enjoy clever wordplay, jokes, and witty repartee. Light and breezy, they'll never come on too strong, but their amusing observations can be sharp and to the point.

Communication is Gemini's middle name, and this could be a great bonus when something's bothering you. Just talk about it. You'll find he's a good listener and very adaptable to your needs and desires.

Geminis live in the moment and are always alive in the present split-second. They may therefore be changeable and are often unpredictable. They can be restless, moody, or even contradictory at times—scintillating in the morning and depressed by mid-afternoon—so get used to the emotional roller coaster. Their constantly moving, busy minds can forget that promise; it's easy for a Gemini husband to say, "I don't remember saying I'd *definitely* finish cleaning out the closet today."

Geminis usually do remain somewhat cool and detached. You can get to know a Gemini very easily, but to really get inside the Gemini heart, mind, and soul is a very difficult thing indeed—something only a wife and a select few will succeed in doing.

These people can do just about anything. Their talents are multitudinous, and they know a little about just about everything. From fixing the drain to knowing how to handle a difficult neighbor, they are up to any challenge, as long as it can be resolved quickly!

Geminis also know an awful lot about the world around them. This communicator knows the personalities, eccentricities, talents, and histories of 101 friends, neighbors, and associates. Need to ask the super of the building for a favor but don't know how best to approach this key person? Ask your husband. You'll find that he'll probably already be on a first-name basis with him, even though you yourself have hardly spoken to him!

Geminis are quick-witted and personable, the perfect people to take along to professional get-togethers or awkward family gatherings. They can easily entertain clients, customers, and relatives and will speak intelligently on a wide range of topics.

You'll usually find it easy to cooperate with him. Geminis don't generally make a big deal about anything and will agree to go along with something you feel strongly about. Their intelligent and objective point of view will always provide a rational take on the subject or problem at hand. They can come up with any number of suggestions or solutions to a particular problem and will play devil's advocate to discuss the pros and cons of each. But your new husband may be so sharp and quick-witted that it's hard to out-talk him. He'll effortlessly change the subject or even his own mind. If you need to air your views, it could help to take him out for a drive or a walk in the park. Appeal to logic and avoid accusations.

Because a Gemini is easily bored and likes the stimulation of the new, he may prove to be unreliable on long-term independent projects. Always check up on his progress and don't hesitate to remind him! It can help to actually sit down together to clean out the closet or get your taxes organized. Some people of this sign are more reliable and grounded than others; you'll just have to know your particular Gemini well to find out for yourself.

You fell in love with him because he was so delightfully easy to talk to, but Geminis can talk too much. You may find your husband prefers to chatter aimlessly rather than do almost anything else, and will go around in circles with a multitude of alternative ideas while avoiding a decision. Yet Geminis are not usually forceful, and gentle nudgings should settle them down. Or perhaps your husband is simply bored. If this is the case, try to split up the responsibilities to make it more interesting to the Gemini temperament. Most will love phone calls, talking to others, seeking new information, or writing. And they must have variety above all else. Be sure to leave your regular routine outside the bedroom. Your guy responds to verbal cues: phone sex or a spicy text message at work can heat him up for the evening or a big weekend ahead.

Geminis are for the most part so likeable that you'll forgive your man most of his faults. Like a breath of fresh air, a Gemini can turn a boring day into a party. This sign knows that life shouldn't be taken too seriously. Accept the twins as they are. Don't be upset if they say nothing one morning when they're in a mood, and don't pin them down or restrain their effervescent spirits too much. You'll find you'll have a stimulating partner, an entertaining cohort, and an endless supply of information in your Gemini husband. Have fun!

### Positives

Geminis are easy to talk to and be with. These men are just plain charming, and they like to keep it light. Because they're interested in what you're doing and thinking, there's usually a natural give-and-take.

### Negatives

While Geminis always need to be in close relationships, they also need many friends. If you're the jealous or possessive type, you'll have to get used to his chatting with other women sometimes.

## YOUR GEMINI IN-LAWS

Gemini in-laws are charming and lively. The twinkle in their eyes and the smiles on their faces reveal perpetual youth. They're curious about everything in the world around them and may even be trivia addicts. They're easy to be with and to talk to. You may be surprised to find just how many varied interests your Gemini in-laws have—book clubs, home repair, and gardening or crafts are a typical few. They can be perpetual students, avidly taking adult education courses like belly dancing or weight training after the age of fifty. You're sure to find something in common to share.

Geminis are flexible and live in the moment. They won't be upset by changes in plans or schedules. But they can potentially be flaky at times, too, so be sure to call to remind them of your anniversary dinner party before they're whisked away to another adventure.

Geminis are terrific conversationalists. Call up your Gemini mother-in-law when you're feeling down or just want to chat. She'll make keeping in touch seem effortless and will easily share her lighthearted spirits.

While often not the most emotional of parents, Geminis are friendly folks who aren't likely to interfere with your life with your new husband. And who can really ask for more than that?

## YOUR GEMINI MAID OF HONOR

A Gemini maid of honor easily understands exactly what all the brides-maids and family members are up to. She'll chat with one, argue with another, and find out exactly what's being done. She'll keep you up to date on the what, where, when, and how of your wedding.

Don't let the Gemini inquisitive streak fool you into thinking she's a control freak. Geminis adapt to what everyone can deliver and let you work without restriction or pressure. These smart folks know better than to try to change you. Responsibility or long hours finalizing projects are not for this maid of honor, who will prefer to have other trusted brides-maids handle them. She's better suited to evaluate proposals and come up with new ideas than to sit doggedly at a desk juggling your budget.

Geminis can change their minds, moods, and ideas too quickly for others to keep up. You may find that your maid of honor routinely re-schedules the shower or bachelorette party, but you'll probably be more disconcerted when your rehearsal dinner seems next on the hit list! Changes are no big deal to a Gemini. She'll be keeping up with current developments. But if you're like those of us who become attached to regular ways of doing things, you'll just have to slow her down.

It might be difficult to get this maid of honor's undivided attention. Phone calls, other people popping in, and other thoughts that come to her mind can all interfere. Get the most out of your time together by clearly outlining the issues at hand and getting right to the important facts. Be clear, concise, and entertaining when you can, the better to keep the Gemini attention. If you have an interesting problem to solve, your maid of honor may become so involved that she'll actually handle it for you in about half the time it would've otherwise taken.

Don't be put off by double talk. If your maid of honor wants to avoid a subject, there are a multitude of ways she'll do this. You may be agreeing it's not a good idea to shop for dresses at all before you realize it! Keep your wits about you and keep to the subject at hand.

For all their potential inconsistencies, Gemini maids of honor are easy to work with. Add to that an entertaining, charming personality and a lighthearted attitude, and you'll probably agree to keep this woman among your best of friends.

# CHAPTER 16

# Cancer

## (JUNE 21–JULY 22)

Emotional and sensitive, Cancer men are attached to their homes and families. They think with their hearts and trust their gut feelings. Tender and sentimental, Cancerians are often the ones who remember birthdays and anniversaries, even when you forget. They're lovers of home and family who'll nurture you with affection, waffles, and a homemade latte. They're sensitive, though, and don't always keep their emotions (or calories!) in check.

# YOUR CANCER HUSBAND

Affectionate and sentimental, the Cancer husband is not the typical macho man. He's warm and caring and not afraid to show his feelings. Sometimes shy and retiring with strangers, this is the kind of guy who knows what intimacy is all about—and he strives for it.

Get him a sweet, sappy card for his birthday or make him his favorite dessert, and he'll be touched to the core. But be aware that he's more sensitive than most men. He needs sympathy and understanding and may need to pour out his heart from time to time. Be there to listen and soothe his spirits, and you'll be well on your way to the kind of marriage many women only dream about.

Show your affection: kiss your Cancer guy and tell him how much you care! You can also put him in a romantic mood by making him comfort food or taking him out for ice cream. Or dress yourself up with whipped cream and *be* the dessert!

You'll avoid a lot of hurt feelings and misunderstandings if you remember that these people are very sensitive emotionally, at times overly so. Cancerians can appear standoffish or even cold when they're upset—they'll withdraw into their emotional shells. Or they can yell and scream to beat the band. Most men in our society aren't taught how to deal with their emotions effectively, and it's especially difficult for Cancer men, as they're so very emotional. Your husband might be up one minute and depressed the next; it could be impossible to predict his emotional swings. If you can avoid being influenced by this behavior, so much the better. Encourage him toward evenness with your own consistent upbeat attitude.

Cancer men take everything too personally. If you must argue with yours, try to remain calm and understanding. Be sure to say, "I feel reined in" rather than "You're too clingy!" and don't deny or reject his feelings.

As Cancerians live in the emotional world, they often have accurate impressions of others. You may think Neighbor X is jovial and hardworking, but your husband can tell you right away he's a blowhard and slipshod, something you won't find out for several months. His gut instincts may be exaggerated, but they're often right on target.

Your Cancer husband is a collector: of facts, memories, and things as well as people. Most Cancerians will keep the fridge well stocked and hang onto a good job. But this collect-a-mania can pose problems too. So much stuff! His closets, drawers, and desk will be loaded with things that you might view as junk or garbage. He won't want to throw anything out and may overflow onto surrounding areas with files, piles, boxes, and bags of...who knows what? Well, whatever it is, it's extremely important to the Cancer guy, who will be quite upset at any aggressive attempts on your part to do away with it. He'll appreciate, instead, your ideas for good storage space.

Try to sugarcoat any direct criticism, as Cancerians are extremely sensitive to anything that will make them feel ridiculed. But Cancer people think that everyone else is as sensitive as they are, so they'll go out of their way to show their own support of you.

Cancer men are excellent providers. They seem to have inherited a survival instinct from their ancestors and make good use of it. Often ambitious, but in a quiet way, they're terrific savers. No matter how much your income, a Cancer husband will usually put a little away each week. Security is important to him, and he'll plan to own a home too.

Cancer is the big homebody of the zodiac, and family is a priority for him. He'll be happy to help around the house and spend time shopping. Cancerians are usually interested in having children and make great fathers. A Cancer husband may prefer you to stay home with the kids, but he's adaptable to your needs as well. If parenting is a priority of yours, be assured he'll share it.

Cancer people are the comfort foodies of the zodiac. They love to eat and often crave sweets. That's fine if he's fit, but many can also be couch potatoes who don't enjoy working out or vigorous physical activity. You can more easily get him to eat healthfully by sharing meals with him or going grocery shopping together. If he doesn't have a gallon of ice cream in the freezer, he'll be less likely to overindulge!

Unhappy Cancerians make miserable partners. They can brood, drag around, and idle away time gazing out a window or into open space. They need to keep in touch with their families and may spend endless hours on the phone if they're in crisis mode or when significant others are feeling low. Remind him gently that you need his attention and offer some advice on his problems. Cancerians are always much more cooperative with those they feel warmly toward. He'll feel warmly toward you if you give him emotional support and personal attention.

If you're married to a Cancer with a negative attitude, or if you're not doing your share of the household chores, be prepared for some steady and tortuous nagging. Cancerians can complain ad infinitum when in discomfort or upset. They'll nag and harp at you until you do what you're supposed to or what they feel you should. It is a little childish but usually has the intended result; you'll eventually say, "I'll do it, I'll do it, just shut up already!" Forceful and direct Aries, Leo, and Sagittarius people should especially avoid losing their tempers with a Cancer husband. He'll be upset for a long time to come, and you'll have further problems dealing with him. A sweet, syrupy apology can go a long way.

So be nice. Be diplomatic. Be *sensitive*. You've got a man who is warm, generous, supportive, and loyal. And among all those piles that you thought were junk, your husband will be able to dig out just the thing that you tossed last month and now desperately need.

### Positives

Warm and mushy, once he has you, he likes to hold on. He'll listen to your problems and bring you chicken soup if you have a cold.

### Negatives

He could be moody, oversensitive, and easily hurt. When he's upset, he can lose his temper or just brood and close off.

## YOUR CANCER IN-LAWS

That chubby, chocolate-chomping in-law who was so reticent at first could well be a Cancer. These folks may be a little quiet or shy until you're better acquainted. They're usually sweet, sentimental people who will cling to their "little boy" for the rest of his life, providing emotional and even financial support to you and your family. They're easy to get to know once you know a secret: they adore talking about their son and other family members. Cancerians collect memories, photos, and other stuff of the family's past. If you join them in exploring their basement, garage, or genealogy and listen to their stories, you're sure to win their hearts.

They're fond of all family gatherings and they *will* want grandchildren! If this is not on your immediate agenda, tell them so, politely but firmly. They can be persistent naggers, so stand strong!

Cancer in-laws may be clingy and may not give up the monopoly they've enjoyed over their son's attention so easily. Be patient with them and go slow in changing your husband's habits with his family. These in-laws might be moody or even snappish at times. Don't take it personally. Soothe them, be calm and cool, and you're sure to have an in-law you would love to have as your own parent.

## YOUR CANCER MAID OF HONOR

Cancer maids of honor are wonderfully sympathetic and caring, and they can have insight into the thoughts and feelings of those around them. While they may at times appear childlike, they will act the parent role the rest of the time. If you need help, you'll be taken care of. The Cancer maid of honor can be downright motherly, making sure everyone is feeling right, eating right, and taking care of business. She may be especially gifted in helping select caterers and choose dresses, as food and clothing are Cancerian specialties.

Cancerians empathize with personal feelings and obligations. If it's easier to have her handle your in-laws, just ask. There's usually no need to make up an outrageous lie for a Cancer maid of honor. If you can't bear to face your ex but desperately want the book of poetry you left at his apartment three years ago, she'll probably also take care of it.

Cancerians will take charge in a quiet way. They don't order others about; that isn't their style. They're looking to help you with your wedding in the most efficient way possible. But a Cancerian could resort to nagging and carping. She may also complain about the other bridesmaids, and you might at times feel torn in your loyalties. Be as sympathetic as you can, but be careful how far you go in intervening in problems of this type. Grace and diplomacy are generally needed in working with a Cancerian to come to a joint decision. Appeal to Cancer's sympathy, emotions, and feelings.

Cancerian maids of honor are notorious penny-pinchers, so if you're a spender, she'll help keep you in line. She'll retrench and go "lean and mean" before she lets you lose any money.

Your Cancer friend can let her feelings get the better of her. She may break down in tears if you snap at her for not picking up the invitations on time. If an upset Cancer isn't crying or throwing a tantrum, she'll probably be brooding or sulking in remote silence. Don't press issues that seem to aggravate her or you'll be the one to ignite the fuse. Try at all times to keep up a pleasant demeanor and helpful manner.

Your Cancer maid of honor, though, is generally a supportive member of the team. The atmosphere can get a little dicey at times, but in the long run you'll have an individual who deeply cares about you. And you'll probably also have a close, caring friend for many years to come.

# CHAPTER 17

## (JULY 23–AUGUST 22)

Leo men love big gestures and big gifts. Their pride in their spouses, houses, and children is boundless—to be shared with anyone who will listen! A Leo may demand attention, but he'll also be there when you need him.

## YOUR LEO HUSBAND

The Leo man is probably good-looking and knows how to dress; you won't see him in sweatpants unless he's working out. He also knows how to relax and have a good time. Marry a Leo man, and you'll get used to going out to the theater, concerts, sporting events, even amusement parks. He's the life of every party and is as comfortable in a crowd as in a one-on-one. Leos can indulge in socializing and gossip—the excitement and drama of these activities is what attracts them. Even the hardest-working Leo will often enjoy going out for lunch, dinner, and drinks.

A Leo man knows who he is and what he wants and is up-front about his feelings. Most are comfortable with displays of affection, in public or private! They're loyal and generous, sometimes to a fault. But don't let him get the idea that he's the king and you're his subject. He may find taking out the trash demeaning, but he'll do it if he understands it's a gift he's contributing to the marriage. And don't forget "thank you"—your praise and compliments will help him make a great relationship even better!

Warm, outgoing, and gregarious, Leos tend to put emphasis on appearances. He'll want you to look good when you go out—the better to show you off! These people often judge others from the very appearance of things; subtle power struggles may be beyond their understanding. Outgoing and confident, they always need to prove that they're important, vital, and in control. They also have a real flair for the dramatic, able to make even the most insignificant trip to the deli for a sandwich sound like an epic adventure when retold.

Open and straightforward, your husband won't plot, scheme, or hold grudges against you. He generally does mean well, wants to be loved, and is a real softie at heart. If you apologize for a mistake, he's so magnanimous he can't help but forgive and forget...even if he still does believe you were wrong!

You must have noticed that your Leo likes to talk about himself—and that this can at times be the only topic of conversation! You may have to interrupt forcefully to get in your side of the story, but Leo mates will soon return to their point of view. Although discussions may be somewhat one-sided, if you're firm and stick to what you've got to say, you'll end up in a lively discussion.

People of this sign like to stick to their guns. They'll rise to the challenge of tough competition, so your lively discussion could eventually get out of hand, especially if you're another stubborn sign like Taurus, Scorpio, or Aquarius. Leos often have a hard time understanding other people's points of view. Although aggravated by continued opposition, they actually also enjoy this kind of sporting showdown. They are tenacious and are willing to wait for solutions.

Probably the most successful way around a stubborn Leo husband is to appeal to his good nature. Don't try to win a sparring match with him; instead, put your heads together and brainstorm solutions. Meeting halfway is difficult for a Leo, but if you can allow him to save face by utilizing some of his key points, it'll go a long way toward a compromise. Your lion may tend to roar when angry, but with time he can be trained to be a good sport who works things out with mutual respect.

Try to get around direct opposition from your husband by emphasizing observations like "Your thinking is always so thorough" or "You usually know what's right" before coming to the big "but maybe we can do it my way." A Leo doesn't like to let go of a problem until it's solved. If you genuinely try to work things out in a loving manner, you're more likely to be successful with him.

Signs like Aries, Sagittarius, and Aquarius have their own points of honor and will not want to stoop to manipulations of flattery and admiration, but they are the only surefire ways to the lion's heart. Suffice it to say that if you do appreciate and admire your Leo husband, don't hesitate to say so! These people love and need recognition, acceptance, and support. If you like them, they'll like you—it's really that simple.

Compliments will get you everywhere. Tell him how gorgeous his haircut looks or how incredible he makes you feel in bed, and he won't be able to resist. He also loves entertainment, so take him out for a splashy night on the town. PDAs will prime him for a thrilling evening back home. Leos are typically generous souls who will give gifts and spend freely. They're lovers at heart who'll keep the romance in your marriage going strong long after the honeymoon is over.

Leos also like to tell others what to do, and this can be hard to take sometimes. He just can't see why you wouldn't always want to do things *his* way! Try to make light of this whenever possible, and explain your own point of view in clear and straightforward terms. While you could eventually find the lion's nudgings irritating or even obnoxious, remember that your husband is only trying to help you.

Many Leo men have lazy streaks, but they'll dive enthusiastically into special projects that they enjoy. He might love to barbecue, play with kids, fix the car, or do creative tasks like building a deck or going shopping for furniture. But if your Leo guy hates the project or doesn't want to do his share of the household chores, he might spend much of your time chatting about windsurfing, last week's lunch with the boss, or the attributes of the latest celebrity cologne. Try appealing to the lion's innate pride in these cases. A negative Leo could call you "no fun" or a "bad sport," but he'll feel bad if he knows he's disappointed you.

He may talk too much, he may at times be lazy, but a Leo husband will certainly add zest and fun to life. Your home and your heart would be emptier without him!

### Positives

A Leo is loyal and honest, with a good heart. This man is romantic and knows how to make a date great.

### Negatives

Leo men have huge egos, and they think they're always right. They can be stubborn and may try to be the boss in the relationship. Appearances can be too important to them.

## YOUR LEO IN-LAWS

You were probably charmed to meet your Leo in-law. Dinner seemed effortless as the Leo shared personal stories and lively anecdotes. But by the third course, you may have tired of the show. Leos love to be the center of attention, and you're now a permanent part of the audience! It will help if you find things in common. Leos are often fun-loving people who are up on the latest movies, celebrities, and current events.

Leos usually take special pride in their children. You may have to take a back seat to their attentions toward their splendid son, though more affectionate Leos (especially those without girls of their own) might adopt you.

Some Leos may be too busy with their own lives and careers to take much time with yours. They won't be shy about demanding your attention and commanding your appearance when it suits their mood or schedule. Leos are used to telling others what to do, especially their children. They may be bewildered that your husband now has other priorities.

Older and retired Leos will have more time and will love to sit with your kids or help you plan a birthday party. They often mellow and become more affectionate, attached, and supportive of you as they age. Enjoy it!

## YOUR LEO MAID OF HONOR

The Leo maid of honor can be magnanimous and generous with both her time and the wedding budget. A good Leo maid of honor delegates responsibility, infuses others with enthusiasm, and receives genuine admiration and respect. She's naturally a terrific hostess and party planner, and she'll see to it that everyone has a great time. While she won't enjoy taking second stage, she'll bask in your reflected glow and take great pride in her role as your greatest friend.

Leos like to give advice. If you're having a problem and honestly want to solve it, a Leo is your perfect foil. Supportive, protective, and encouraging, she'll be a strong advocate for your wants and needs with your family, guests, and even fiancé.

If Leo maids of honor don't feel they're getting the proper respect from others, they'll be unhappy. Show your own respect, deference, and appreciation. If you disagree, arrange for a private interview and be tactful but open in your discussion. Your Leo maid of honor will appreciate that you had enough honesty to discuss the matter in a dignified manner.

An ambitious and driven Leo maid of honor will work you hard and demand excellence. She may at times produce a stifling atmosphere by taking too much control. Yes, she could ask the bridesmaids to do things that she wouldn't do herself, but she'll never ask them to do something she doesn't believe in. And even the most hopeless attendant will be given a second chance if a Leo really believes she's honestly trying to give it her all.

Your Leo maid of honor will not be shy about expressing her disgust if she feels an attendant has been ungenerous or unfair. Even you could be the victim of her annoyance. She'll find it more chivalrous if you admit a mistake and promise to do better than if you try to make excuses.

Sometimes positions of authority bring out the negative side of Leo. She may become egotistical and vain, demanding that things go her way and treating others with condescension. She might play favorites and could be swayed by flatterers while being oblivious to the faults of those she likes. Some Leo maids of honor can also rest at the top and let everyone else do all the work.

Usually, though, the generous and loving side of a Leo maid of honor predominates. Kind and warm by nature, she easily combines showing affection with producing an elegant affair. If you remember that your Leo friend would really rather be the queen of the ball, you'll get along just fine!

# CHAPTER 18

# Virgo

## (AUGUST 23–SEPTEMBER 22)

Virgo men have high standards and don't marry just anyone. Generally quiet and hardworking, your Virgo keeps himself busy. He's so thoughtful! He'll run out for cough syrup and lozenges when you have a cold.

## YOUR VIRGO HUSBAND

Are any husbands really happy to scrub the bathroom tile or vacuum the living room? Just a few, and usually they're Virgos! These men hate clutter. If it's not your thing to clean, a Virgo will quickly take over. He's a kind, caring soul who won't put on airs or show off. This is a man who will cheerfully take care of everything when you're feeling down. He's also pretty expert at changing diapers!

Virgo men are hard workers, and their careers are often important to them. Your husband needs to feel he has a purpose in life, but he can overdo it. If he starts working long, stressful hours, you may have to intervene—he understands that saving his energy for you is important too.

Your Virgo husband is quite prudent about his health and hygiene. He may brush and floss his teeth in the office washroom after lunch and can stay home at the first hint of a cold. But this common sense extends to his work, one of the few things that are of equal importance to Virgos.

Virgos are very responsible about the duties entrusted to them and will put in a lot of time and effort to try to get things done to perfection. Likeable companions, they're often helpful and supportive. They tend to be quiet and reserved, as they put more emphasis on work than on socializing. But what to do with a guy whose idea of a hot date is booting up TurboTax or watching CNN together? Pamper him by sharing a long, relaxing break in a hot tub. He needs peace and quiet and loves nature and pets. Getting down to earth with your Virgo guy will probably soothe your jangled nerves as well. Sharing aromatherapy candles or a romantic comedy together can put him in the mood for love. But don't come on too strong and send your panties to him at work! He'll freak out.

Modest and unassuming (some are even shy), you'll find your Virgo husband a charming, witty conversationalist. He'll have an excellent mind and can be quite discriminating. He has the ability to see people, things, and situations for what they really are. Trappings, clever facades, and "put on" affectations will never fool a bright Virgo who knows who's who and what's what and is always a realist.

These men are good at analysis, have excellent perception, and notice even the smallest details. Nothing will escape their keen observations and scrutiny. They have wry senses of humor. More often, though, their criticisms and summations of people and situations are so right-on and frank that they inspire laughter without ever intending to. Simple, concise, and personally felt, Virgos have a knack for understating the obvious.

Virgos will routinely speak up to offer suggestions and criticism. This is one of their few real compulsions: they're so keenly aware of trying to improve that they want to get you to do your best as well. Although the delivery may not always be pleasant, Virgo criticism is generally meant to be constructive. Try to overlook the fact that the advice was unsolicited. If you have a more sensitive disposition, take solace in the knowledge that your Virgo means well, and realize that his comments are far from personal.

You may be stunned by your Virgo husband's critical barbs, which can fly in the midst of an argument. Your best armor is a calm control of the facts. Keep negotiations with this sometimes high-strung man cool and sensible. Avoid judgments and you'll keep your arguments on the right track.

There's real value in Virgo's observations, and if you can be objective and take some of his advice, you'll often find it fruitful. If you're hopelessly lost in a messy desk, disorganized routine, or red tape, ask him to help sort things out. He'll be happy to do so, and you'll soon realize how easy it is to maintain orderly habits. Virgos understand how little things can add up to big results.

Some Virgos can be walking drugstores, supremely intent on maintaining their health. Besides the toothbrush and toothpaste, they may carry around a first aid kit, ibuprofen (never aspirin—too hard on the stomach), antacid, vitamins, breath mints, and laxatives. Now you don't have to worry if you ever need these items! He might also keep a sewing kit, safety pins, and a change of underwear and socks in the glove compartment of his car, just in case.

Perhaps his greatest strength is in knowing how to help those in need. Virgos handle emergencies with the same calm composure they do everything else. In times of crisis, he'll come through and save the day with his dedication and know-how. Depend on him to be there when you need him.

These people are true helpmates. They're adaptable, will plunge in to do their best, and will follow if you take the lead. Your husband will always do his share, if not more than that. If you're tiling the kitchen together, he'll be organized and systematic about getting the job done.

But gird yourself for some practical advice and criticism. You may not be putting the tiles in the precisely correct position! A Virgo will be vocal but will never be pushy; although he may feel disgruntled with what he perceives as sloppiness or incomplete work, he usually won't provoke a big conflict.

Virgo people strive for perfection, and some can get carried away with it. If you're married to a finicky Virgo who insists on chewing each bite twenty times or constantly rolling a lint brush over his suit, it could be time to put your foot down. Overemphasis on perfection can become inefficiency, and you just might point this out gently to your Virgo mate. Or give him a practical talk about how difficult it is to attain perfection in the material world. (Make sure it's a practical talk, as Virgos have no use for philosophy.)

Because of their dedicated, hardworking natures, Virgos make better husbands than many others. Follow his example if you can: Virgo is the most service-oriented sign of the zodiac. If you've married one, you'll have the extra bonus of great diet and exercise advice whenever you need it!

Positives

A Virgo has both feet on the ground and knows what he wants. He'll help you out, find you a job, and even volunteer to take out the trash.

Negatives

This guy has a nervous side and can worry too much. His activities may be more important to him than enjoying life. He could be critical of how you look, dress, or express yourself.

## YOUR VIRGO IN-LAWS

Your Virgo in-laws may still be wearing the overcoats they bought five years ago, but you can bet they were a fantastic value, in a timeless style, and are still in tip-top condition.

Virgos are often concerned with health, and you may be treated to the details of their colonoscopy or their dentist's thoughts about the new bridge. But they'll take an interest in your own health and are usually proactive about caring for their own. Virgos are sensitive to their bodies but are nevertheless often hardy souls.

They strive to do things properly, and you'll rarely see one with a tie askew or scuffed shoes. These are the people who'll straighten a painting on your wall or pluck a loose hair from your shoulder.

But they're good listeners and are helpful people in general. A Virgo will do the laundry if you're sick in bed and mop the floor if you need that done too. Not even picking up dog poop or cleaning the toilet grosses them out.

The gifts they give will not be showy, but you'll probably find that you use that corkscrew or pajamas they gave you all the time. A Virgo in-law will support your life. Isn't that nice?

## YOUR VIRGO MAID OF HONOR

A Virgo maid of honor is a capable manager who concentrates on the details in order to attain results. Bit by bit, in a methodical way, she'll see to it that everyone is working effectively and efficiently to create a lovely event.

The neatness, orderliness, and cleanliness of your maid of honor's home and dress tell you a lot about the inner person. Virgos are organized and efficient to a fault. Practical, down-to-earth, and industrious, they set fine examples because they'll work harder and accomplish more than they'll ever expect you to. Your maid of honor takes her duties seriously.

Listen to the advice and criticisms of your Virgo friend. Try to understand exactly what she thinks you should change and why. Leave your ego at home: she's usually up-front and honest and is only helping you to be your best. If you can take her criticism constructively, you'll be on your way to having a more elegant affair.

A Virgo loves facts! She knows how to get good quality for value, instinctively understanding which beading will tend to fall off and which is expertly sewn. She'll think things through and won't rush herself, double-checking all that she does for minute errors. She can have the catering hall estimate in hand in a minute. Could you do the same? You may choose to leave her in charge of the organization of bills, records, and so on. She'll pack your bag for you or suggest "must have" items to take on your honeymoon.

You may have to help your Virgo maid of honor delegate responsibility—she could tend to feel no one will do as good a job a she does and may take on too much. A Virgo is there to serve your needs. If you're in a real jam, she'll do all she can to help, including taking on more duties. Be sure to get together for down time when the two of you can just relax without discussing the wedding.

There are a lot of little things that your Virgo maid of honor will focus on. But if you pay attention to them, the big things will take care of themselves. You won't get praise or kudos from this maid of honor for doing what's expected of you. But you'll get deference to your needs and the rewards of knowing that you've pulled off the loveliest affair possible. What more can you realistically ask for?

# CHAPTER 19

# Libra

## (SEPTEMBER 23–OCTOBER 22)

Lively and outgoing, the Libra man has a charm and sweetness that make him likeable. Popular and easy to talk to, a Libra relishes his spouse's point of view and is expert at cooperation.

## YOUR LIBRA HUSBAND

Libra is the sign of partnership, and Libra men really do like to be married. They understand the give-and-take necessary to a good relationship, and they're cooperative and understanding. Your husband will respect your wishes and be happy for you to take the lead when you need or want to.

A Libra man is first and foremost a classy guy. You can count on him to be sociable and have good manners, and you can also trust him to behave appropriately no matter where you go. He'd much prefer a heart-to-heart discussion to an argument and will strive for domestic peace and tranquility. Libras are idealistic rather than emotional. If you have a difference of opinion, your Libra will try hard to work out a compromise that's agreeable to both of you—it just might take him a while to get there. Libras are notorious for their slow decision-making, so learn to love the process as much as you love the guy!

Libra men are usually elegant and sophisticated, dressing in lovely colors and with good taste while remaining beautifully conservative. They avoid the flashy, trendy, and plain in favor of pleasing combinations and tastefully appropriate dress.

Even their small talk and idle chitchat have a likeability and pleasance that goes far beyond content. Libras concentrate on the "how" and make it always "with decorum." They can talk a lot but are also good listeners, as they instinctively know that balance between two people results in a good relationship.

Librans need to have people around. They're charming companions and conversationalists who know just the right thing to say at awkward moments. So the waiter just spilled a whole bowl of pasta Bolognese in your mother's lap? Don't worry! Your Libra husband will smooth over the event with such finesse and tact that Mom will probably remember it as an interlude from Fellini's *Roma* rather than the most embarrassing and painful moment of your relationship.

These are the "Have a good day" people. And even if you think that saying that phrase is insipid or empty, there's certainly nothing offensive, rude, or difficult about it. And yes, it can cheer you up and make you smile too. Which man would you rather come home to: the one who says, "Have a nice day" or the one who mutters, "I guess I'll see ya later"?

Libras are cautious not to upset, offend, or ruffle anyone's feathers. If you're busy and can't talk, just say so. He'll back off politely and won't take it personally. Understanding and considerate, he has the ability to adjust to your needs. He won't be aggressive or pushy and knows how to work at relationships.

Stimulate him with sophisticated enjoyments, then soothe his senses with subtle pleasures. Treat him to the opera or a gallery opening; go for a gourmet meal and dancing. Then savor the memory, queue up a Norah Jones album, and dim the lights.

Do you understand him yet? Think the "pleasure principle": Libras prefer things that are nice and trouble-free. He may try to avoid unpleasant, uncomfortable, or distasteful situations. A mature man born under this sign will attempt to make a difficult situation less so by putting up a good front, taking an optimistic attitude, and playing fair. He'll strive to create a supportive, stress-free, and attractive atmosphere.

Librans can help disparate factions come together. They believe in the benefits of negotiation and diplomacy and are objective in their views. This makes them wonderful to live with. When teaming up with a Libra, expect to have your talents utilized and your flaws artfully minimized.

Yet Libras often can't and won't be forceful, lose tempers, or make scenes. If any or all of these things seem necessary, don't expect your Libra to do it! Sometimes, and with certain people, a strong sentiment needs to be expressed in order to get results, but this is not typical. Co-operate with your Libra by being polite, considerate, and kind; he's sensitive and easily thrown off balance. Approach him on his own terms if you want results.

Anger just doesn't work with these people. While Librans may at times appear to be "yea-sayers," these individuals will not let themselves be pushed into decisions or actions by force. They will politely ease themselves out of any situation they feel is too sticky. If peace talks fail, stay squarely on message. Emotional fireworks may lead your husband to implode. Appeal to his innate fairness and cooperative nature. But remember that his idea of fairness and yours may be different. Talk about that too!

Libras can also be indecisive as a result of their need to consider all points of view. If you're decisive yourself, you'll probably work well together. But expect a list of pros and cons if you ask your husband's opinion. Libra relies on the process of balancing views. You may need to cut this short due to deadlines or your own impatience.

Remember that your Libra husband needs to maintain balance at all costs. He'll compromise, but may stubbornly go to great lengths to guarantee behavior and decisions that he feels will be the best for both of you. But a Libra can make practically anything sound as if it's the best for both of you! If you disagree with him, speak up.

It may also be difficult to understand what these likeable people are really feeling. They don't often let down their guard and will try to maintain a good relationship with the most difficult of family members. Ultimately, who cares if he's always completely genuine as long as the relationship is working?

Some Librans are such pleasure seekers that they don't like to work. They'll focus on their love life (a plus for you!), spending money, and surrounding themselves with beautiful people and things. If you need to bring one of these reluctant types down to earth, use reasoning, the concept of fairness, and a polite but firm attitude to get results.

Libras in general, though, do more good than harm. And just like the "Have a nice day" cashier, they can often be relatively harmless when at their worst. At his best, your husband is a sweet, cooperative individual who can be diligent and ambitious when completing projects for the benefit of all concerned. And he's also the prefect person to be your better half!

### Positives
This man really wants a relationship! He's responsive to your needs and knows how to compromise. He'll make a great impression on your family.

### Negatives
A Libra may tend to get too involved in other people's lives. Indecision haunts him, and he could have trouble making up his mind.

## YOUR LIBRA IN-LAWS

You should be aware of the things that Librans do best: look good, sound good, and make others feel good. They're civilized. As long as you behave in a cordial manner, you'll get along well with them.

Libras gravitate toward people who represent their ideal: well-spoken, emotionally in control, polite individuals. If you want to be truly accepted by your Libra in-law, you may have to "class up" a little. Don't raise your voice, don't be obviously forceful or aggressive, and couch what you say in a pleasant manner. These may seem insignificant to you, but paying attention to these traits can make all the difference to your Libra in-law. Now that you've gone through this beautifying transformation, in the

Libra view, you'll have the ability to make a pleasing impression as part of the family.

Libra people really do network, negotiate, compromise, and smile their way through the day. The number-one Libra credo is "You must get along with others." Succeeding corollaries are "If she likes to talk to you, she'll talk to you," and "We'll have a better relationship with our son if we like his wife." If you can learn these, too, you'll forge a terrific bond.

## YOUR LIBRA MAID OF HONOR

Firm but always fair, a Libra maid of honor will treat you as a partner in your wedding planning. She'll combine your talents with those of your family and attendants to get the wedding accomplished smoothly.

Libra maids of honor are some of the most polite, well mannered, and well meaning of attendants. The relationship is the important thing! Libras wait, weigh, compromise, and negotiate. Although Libras usually get what they want in the end, others won't ever know it since such balanced views were expressed and fairness for all concerned seemed to be the most important issue.

Libras know all about beauty. Your maid of honor will help you cultivate an attractive appearance, seeing that you pay attention to your hair and don't wear too much makeup or jewelry. With her help, you'll look lovely in whatever you wear. She'll get out the etiquette books and share what Ms. Manners has to say about all those traditional niceties that go beyond "please" and "thank you."

Your maid of honor can see both sides of the coin at once. If you think about the mental gymnastics involved in actually doing that, you'll realize why she can take so long to come to a decision. You may at times just have to wait...and wait...and wait. It might be easier for you to take responsibility for some decisions on your own.

More often than not, a Libra maid of honor will be able to calm a jumpy fiancé, cajole a reluctant florist, or sweet-talk a temperamental baker. But Librans may avoid unpleasant dirty work and leave the other attendants to it. If you've got a really self-indulgent Libra maid of honor, all hell can break loose as long as things look good, and many complaints can be made providing she doesn't have to hear them. But there's a way to get a Libra maid of honor to straighten up: force her to see and understand the real unpleasantness that's going on around you. If she has any pride left, things will improve. You may also have to be decisive and implement appropriate action.

But you'll usually have a wonderful atmosphere while working with a Libra, and your attendants, if approved by your Libra maid of honor, will be cooperative and kind as well. All of us can quickly get used to being a little more refined and liking it!

# CHAPTER 20

# Scorpio

## (OCTOBER 23–NOVEMBER 21)

A Scorpio man is mysterious and sexy. Although reserved, he's very intense. Behind his mesmerizing, soulful gaze is a deep lake of molten lava. Though potentially volcanic, these complex creatures value security, and they'll work hard to provide stability for a family.

## YOUR SCORPIO HUSBAND

You may have gotten hooked on your Scorpio man at first sight. He's intense about everything he does—from fixing his car to getting involved with you! You already know all about his passionate side. Not just sexual, it's part of his very nature. He'll feel equally strongly about negotiating with his boss, protecting your future kids, or getting the best deal on a mortgage.

Many Scorpios are mystery men who protect their privacy—regardless of whether they have anything to hide. Since you've come this far, he's obviously learned to trust you. Keep it that way by being open and honest—he'll sense it if you're not. But remember, Scorpio men are not the most forthcoming, and it may be painful for your husband to discuss that early failed relationship or his ungrounded suspicions that you still care for someone else. As time goes by, though, you should see him loosening up and becoming more comfortable. Once he learns you really, truly only have eyes for him, you'll become part of his own private space.

Your often-quiet and reserved Scorpio husband certainly doesn't seem to be a walking time bomb, but this is one way of thinking about him. He's full of a tremendous amount of energy, and if it's properly directed, he may never explode. But once you know him long enough, you'll possibly see the fuse ignite. Whether the eruption is big or small depends upon the circumstances, but this behavior can help you understand what Scorpio is all about.

Most often, however, Scorpios are completely in control of their strong emotions. They'd never want it to get out that they care that much! So they play it cool instead of hot and probably have many people fooled into thinking they're detached, disinterested, or uninvolved with the people and events around them. Remember that a Scorpio is by nature reserved—not shy, not insecure, just reserved. Try to let him keep whatever privacy he seems to need.

You may get the impression that your Scorpio husband is self-absorbed. But Scorpio is also quite sensitive and can be overly conscious of his partner on a very deep, almost psychic level. He can perceive and utilize subtle relationships and power struggles, the type of thing that goes unnoticed by most of us. Scorpios are also the kind of people that others either love or hate; they generally don't produce indifference.

Your Scorpio will observe, calculate, and judge before taking action. You'll see how your husband casually places all papers out of sight before leaving his desk. You may get the impression that he leads a double life, being so opaque and secretive. Your husband could change the subject when asked a direct question, or not answer it, though it appears to have been answered with frankness and sincerity. Instead he's really observing you and wondering why you wanted to know that, anyway.

A Scorpio husband will be fiercely protective and become one of the most powerful partners you could have. He'll be ferociously loyal and back you up even when he knows you're wrong. Be patient and kind with this sometimes misunderstood man, and you're sure to keep his lasting regard. Some days your husband may be moody and brooding, and it's best not to pry at these times. If you can distract him with some interesting activities you share, so much the better.

Scorpios are wonderful resources. Need to find out who can help you get something done or details on a family member's character, personal problems, or even love life? Ask your husband. For someone so tight-lipped, you're sure to wonder where this guy came across such intimate and classified information. Scorpios just take a back seat, listen, and learn, often becoming so unobtrusive that others don't even notice.

Though your Scorpio husband may not tell you exactly how he feels, his sexual intensity communicates it clearly. Arouse him with fancy lingerie, his favorite perfume, or hints about your amorous plans in advance. And be sure you find a perfectly private place and plenty of quality time.

Even the nicest Scorpio man can fight dirty sometimes. It's not war— it's *guerrilla* war! He knows your weaknesses and, if necessary, will exploit them. His arsenal includes angry silence and sarcasm. Survive his stinging side by being straightforward and stubborn and sharpening your negotiating skills. Resist his either/or mentality and insist on compromise.

Don't expect an up-front explanation if you can tell by those maybe not-so-subtle signals that you've upset your husband in some way. Scorpios are notorious for not sharing their feelings when they've been hurt and will even lie to avoid an overt showdown. Then they'll take that back seat again and observe some more. But Scorpios don't like to let go of any relationship. If your Scorpio unexpectedly blurts out an oath or yells at you about some minor personal slight, realize that you've really got a close companion. Any expression of personal feeling is not shared lightly, so try to be as sympathetic as possible.

These people may be difficult to cooperate with as they're not really team players and like to take control. Some simply have abrasive personalities. Your Scorpio's views can be dogmatic, and he may be inflexible about what you should be doing or what he'll contribute. "Not my job!" is clearly a Scorpio phrase, and he'll stick to it. Scorpios don't like being pushed but will feel free to push you to do your share. Try to adapt to his attitude or get set for a long-term negotiation toward compromise.

If you can ascertain what's really important to your Scorpio husband, you'll find it a lot easier partnering with this sometimes obsessive individual. Is it letting him have quiet time after work, sharing a drink on the weekend, or sympathizing with his complaints? Don't listen to what he says but observe what he does, and his priorities will soon be clear. When you have a household project to share or family get-together to attend, you'll know what to expect and where your Scorpio won't bend.

If you really want to understand your husband, realize how different he probably is from you, and you'll go a long way toward developing a positive and mutually rewarding relationship.

### Positives

This guy is emotional and passionate. If he's married you, he'll probably do anything for you! He understands all your feelings.

### Negatives

Scorpio men may get possessive and jealous if they see you flirting with someone else. They also tend to be secretive and might not reveal everything about themselves.

## YOUR SCORPIO IN-LAWS

Older Scorpios may appear sweet and quiet. You'll find as time goes by that they are anything but. Intense, often driven individuals, they could have personal charisma but are also complicated people. They have keen insight into others, and you should feel flattered if they adopt you as one of their own.

Perhaps their ulterior motive is learning more about the daily life of their son. You may be met with questions about your personal life and his activities. That's fine if you're open. But many daughters-in-law could be put off by a Scorpio interrogation. Laying down boundaries with these people from the start could be important.

Of course you'll try to be nice, but a Scorpio in-law can see right through a false facade. If you're not genuine and are merely trying to cultivate the Scorpio's affection, you won't be trusted. If for some reason you've invited your in-law's enmity, watch out: it won't be forgotten.

Take any confidences, no matter how small or seemingly insignificant, as important rewards for your loyalty. Your Scorpio in-law will often respect your right to personal feelings and prejudices. If you can exhibit the same behavior and attitude, you'll earn much respect and admiration.

## YOUR SCORPIO MAID OF HONOR

A Scorpio maid of honor can be an angel or a devil and on a day-to-day basis is probably a little of both. She can be powerful or power-hungry. The way she behaves toward you is likely to reflect her personal feelings and current state of mind.

Scorpios are complex and passionate. If you haven't worked closely with your maid of honor before, you might think this is hardly the case. Look a little closer. Isn't she really more open with you than lots of other people? Ever catch her on a very personal call? You were probably surprised at how vulnerable she suddenly seemed.

Yet vulnerable is hardly the word one would apply to this maid of honor when she has a job to do. She'll work hard, sometimes alone all day long without a break, and into the night if necessary. A Scorpio can be quite demanding but won't ever ask the bridesmaids to do anything she wouldn't. The only problem is that she'll do just about anything.

There are different types, of course. Some Scorpios might be more interested in their own personal lives than anything else. This could limit your maid of honor's contributions. Yet the greater number of Scorpios will do everything they can to help a close friend. Personal problems, including illness and domestic or practical matters, never get in the way. Scorpios have an almost superhuman ability to put mind over matter.

Don't raise your voice to your Scorpio maid of honor and don't get into an argument unless you really feel it's necessary. Both may potentially spell disaster. If your maid of honor says there was no problem but continues to behave as if there was one, clue in to the fact that you've just been shut out. Scorpios don't forget slights, no matter how small. You might find at the last moment that she's invited a former flame of yours as her date. But Scorpios never forget kindnesses, either, which can be your greatest asset.

As time goes on, you'll begin to see the inner workings of the Scorpio maid of honor: passion, determination, and commitment. Your warm and loyal friend may be an expert haggler, getting a dressmaker or wedding planner to deliver earlier and more cheaply than you ever thought possible. She might also be the one to schedule a racy bachelorette party or savvy savings-bond shower.

When treated with respect and a healthy dose of compassion, a Scorpio maid of honor can be someone who really gets things done. She'll encourage you to give it your all and make for a wedding you'll never forget.

# CHAPTER 21

# Sagittarius
## (NOVEMBER 22–DECEMBER 21)

Sagittarians are sporty, have lots of friends, and are always on the go. Their optimism and high spirits make them popular. Like knights in shining armor, they have high ideals and a zest for adventure. They may feel hemmed in if they don't have an occasional night out with the guys. Still, Sir Sag loves to brainstorm with you about everything from home improvements to the meaning of life.

# YOUR SAGITTARIUS HUSBAND

Wherever you go, the Sagittarius husband is sure to turn it into a big adventure. Just wait for the honeymoon! He loves going places, meeting new people, and exploring different cultures. You're sure to have a terrific time.

Back at home, you'll find your Sagittarius man to be good-humored, lighthearted, and casual. He's not above telling bathroom jokes or partying down, as he puts his great love of life into everything he does. He's also impulsive and direct, so don't be surprised if you find yourself swept up in his arms when he can't sleep at 3 a.m.!

This man is an idealist and a philosopher at heart, one who truly believes in doing the right thing. He'll happily agree to disagree with you but will always enjoy hearing your side of the discussion.

If his active life ever slows down, he could begin to feel restless; travel often helps. But he'll probably give you plenty of space to pursue your own heart's desire. Most women won't feel tied down by a Sagittarius husband.

Your Sagittarian will usually have a lot to say about the latest personal and world events. You'll love to hear his stories, amusing anecdotes, and adventures, and you'll wonder where he found the time and energy to do so much since he left the house! All you did was have a cold lunch and take a bath. But Sagittarians, after all, have a real zest for life.

A Sagittarian needs to share his ideas and is stimulated by what others have to say. He'll love hanging out at a local poker game with the gang. Often funny, genuine, and right on target in criticism, he can be quite outspoken as well, especially if he feels he's been treated unfairly. Your husband could be bitter about office politics, the national news, or the world situation, as he's idealistic and hates to admit that life may not always be good or fair. Yet he won't let this get in the way of his own behavior, and he'll steadfastly refuse to admit that he could possibly fall victim to manipulations or unseemly gossip. He's right; he probably won't.

A Sagittarian has his own principles, ethics, and morals—a combination of "doing the right thing" and having a lark. Taken to an extreme, this can result in a devil-may-care attitude and might even include his feelings toward the legal system. Sagittarius can be self-righteous at times. But if you believed you lived your life faithfully and truthfully, wouldn't you feel the same way?

Daily life with a Sagittarian will be an adventure: he can introduce you to the wildest exotic restaurant in town or some of his foreign friends. His life is an open book. Before you even felt you knew your Sagittarius well, he probably told you all about his personal life, feelings, and goals. Think twice before you tell your Sagittarius husband anything you'd rather be kept between you, though. Tomorrow the whole neighborhood might know who you think has a bad dye job or how you secretly want to audition for *American Idol*. This man doesn't talk to be obnoxious or spiteful— he just takes joy in everything he hears. Your husband may even repeat some choice comments others have said about you. Don't respond unless you want your own barbed remarks repeated back to their subject! But your Sagittarian husband will honestly be upset if you mention how horrified you are at his indiscretion; it's usually easier for you to exercise a little prudence.

This man loves the exotic. Take him to a Turkish or Thai restaurant, then learn some sex talk in French or Japanese to get his attention. Turn him on by pretending to be two lost souls on a desert island. Be direct and don't forget to have fun!

These people are easy to live with because they're so adaptable: they understand that others have different points of view. If your husband agrees with you on principle, details will never cause a problem. In discussions Sagittarius may digress from the topic at hand, but you can easily get him back on track. In the face of a deadline, he'll enthusiastically give his all to the cause, shopping for delicacies before your big party or sharing discussions with a financial planner. Is he good at these things? That you'll have to figure out for yourself!

Unfortunately, these people don't always follow through with all they've committed to. Remember the wallpapering project your Sagittarius promised to help you with? You'd better, because your husband is likely to forget. He can realize too late that there's an important dinner with your family looming but will really try to do everything possible to keep a promise. If your Sagittarius really does have other commitments, expect a sheepish apology about his forgetfulness. In the end you'll be told frankly what he will or won't do.

If your husband in fact hates polishing floors or doesn't believe in the whole idea to begin with, you'll have a difficult time cajoling him. First of all, you may have a hard time even locating him! Off texting a pal, in a backyard discussion about the existence of God, or taking an extended lunch or coffee break, Sagittarius will avoid the tasks at hand. Even if your husband is where you expect him to be, he may be involved with guests or on a personal call.

This disgruntled guy will probably be snappish and cranky in response to your third reminder for those receipts that you need in order to get on with balancing the checkbook. His response could be an involved argument about why the household isn't organized well enough or how the credit card companies are overcharging their fees. Your husband will probably be candid, too, in sharing your shortcomings, even expounding on how difficult you are to work with.

A Sagittarius enjoys a heated debate and can escalate to yelling, screaming, or even swearing. If this is not your style, engage his philosophical side.

Relate the discussion to larger ideas like truthfulness and integrity, and he should respond in a more positive manner.

In general, though, Sagittarius is more of a charmer than anything else, and if you're not vindictive, any differences between you will be quickly forgotten. Take him out for a drink after work, talk about your legislators, and you'll be on your usual genial footing again.

### Positives

He'll take you to an exotic restaurant, introduce you to new friends, and speed you away on long trips. He loves to talk on the phone and will keep in touch when he's away.

### Negatives

He could overdo it, talking too loud, staying out late, partying too much, or overeating.

## YOUR SAGITTARIUS IN-LAWS

Sagittarius in-laws are genuinely expansive and good-natured. Even if they're not quite as active as they used to be, they'll tell you all about the Nature Channel show or the Ethical Culture lecture they just attended. A Sagittarian can be a devotee of the Dalai Lama, a keen political observer, or significantly involved with a church. Sagittarians are often blunt and outspoken; be sure to take this in a positive frame of mind. And remember that it's in your in-law's nature to forgive and forget and not hold a grudge—don't you do so, either.

In a warm moment of generosity your Sagittarian in-law may enthuse about taking you on a Caribbean cruise or giving you a gift of a rare Incan artifact. However, in the busy Sagittarius day and with such quickly moving minds, these things are often forgotten. Speak up. Don't be shy with this in-law; you'll get nowhere.

These people are light and love keeping in touch—they'll call simply to say "hi." Your in-law will think highly of you if you can discuss books, politics, or current affairs. Brush up on the subjects the Sagittarian is interested in and talk about them! Your in-law will be pleased, and your reputation will soar.

## YOUR SAGITTARIUS MAID OF HONOR

If you've got a Sagittarius maid of honor, you're in luck. This lady is a lot of fun. She may tell jokes and ribald stories and likes to have a good time. You'll never be bored with a Sagittarian by your side. Chores just aren't a grind when working with someone as spontaneous, idealistic, and charming as she is.

Sagittarius is generous to a fault. She's probably thrilled about your upcoming nuptials and will wish you all the best. Really. And you're sure to learn a lot from this bright woman, including her theories of life, international politics, and current events. She might even recommend the latest hot paperbacks or magazines. Unfortunately, none of these may relate to your wedding, and you may need to get her back on track.

The most noticeable quality about your association will be a sense of freedom. This maid of honor doesn't come on heavily and won't be looking over your shoulder as you do your work. Sagittarians are direct and frank. They can't hold back what they really think and would feel dishonest to do so. As a result, you'll have to learn to take such comments as "You look lousy today" with grace.

A Sagittarian maid of honor will likely travel and move around a lot. Capitalize on her love of action by taking her with you to scout venues or explore bridal salons. Usually a wonderful speaker, she can offer an exuberant and heartfelt toast or speech at the rehearsal dinner or reception.

These people are not the greatest at planning ahead. Your maid of honor may suddenly realize that the wedding day is looming and she has to throw things together for the rehearsal dinner. If you're organized, you should periodically update her. Do things yourself or get a more methodical attendant to handle time-sensitive tasks.

Your attention to detail will be very important, as your maid of honor only has an eye for the larger picture. And you could certainly find yourself picking up the pieces at times when the Sagittarius has rushed off or jumped in too quickly.

Cultivate a good sense of humor. Sagittarius loves jokes and silly anecdotes, so share them. Your moods and personal problems will fade when you're with this attendant: Sagittarians are usually cheerful and optimistic and like to surround themselves with liveliness. A winning smile and warm hello for this maid of honor will go a long way in helping both of you work together better.

If you can make up for the Sagittarian's shortcomings, you'll find the rewards of working with this maid of honor are much more than just putting on your wedding together. You'll have a sense of joy and lightness—a wonderful combination for your special day!

# CHAPTER 22

# Capricorn
## (DECEMBER 22–JANUARY 19)

Capricorn men are reserved, and they're usually mature at any age. They know how to plan for the future and work hard to make their dreams come true. Considerate and family oriented, they understand that part of the marriage bargain is making dinner for your parents or babysitting your kid brother.

# YOUR CAPRICORN HUSBAND

Serious, introspective, and mature, the Capricorn man is a realist at heart. He's concerned with practical things like his career and your future together. He can worry and tends to see the downside of life so he'll be prepared for the worst. And he really has a shy side. He may, even at this stage, fear that you won't return his affections, so let him know how much you care.

Time is on your side. Although most Capricorn men will never become gregarious party animals, they live for security. This zodiac sign is made for commitment. Marriage and a family mean much to him, and he'll never take you for granted. He's reliable and responsible and, under that sometimes cool exterior, very sensitive.

A Capricorn man typically works hard and will never do anything to risk the family nest egg. While he could tend to be cheap (he'd call it thrifty), he'll feel comfortable buying things of lasting value, be it a quality car, home, or dishwasher. Your Capricorn husband will be quietly thrilled if you want to brown-bag it for lunch or fix up some leftovers.

Capricorns seem so humble and unassuming that it's hard to believe they're ambitious, but they certainly are in their own nonaggressive way. Your husband might already be planning on being president of the firm some day. And he could well do it through a combination of hard work, respect for authority, and patience, patience, and more patience.

Capricorns are generally quiet and do their share. Naturally serious, they're realists who see things as they are (though some Capricorns become downright pessimists). While people of this sign have a sense of humor, don't expect to see them rolling in the aisles. Capricorns have a dry wit that is usually ironic and may even be cynical. Delivery can be so deadpan that you'll wonder, "Was that supposed to be a joke?" Laugh anyway. It helps to try to loosen him up a bit.

Capricorns are reserved and insecure. They may cover it up with a brusque, businesslike manner, but deep down inside all of them are afraid of being homeless and penniless. Their career drive is just a great need for security at all costs, and they'll take the safest, surest means toward being safe and sound. They won't take risks and are cautious about where they spend their time and effort.

Your Capricorn can be preoccupied with his obligations and will be more sensual when encouraged to relax. It could help to plan a rendezvous in advance. Being openly aggressive might turn him off, so be subtle, consistent, and warm.

Open conflict can overwhelm the worry-prone Capricorn man. His response to verbal ammo may simply be to take cover. Giving him time out from a heated argument will be more persuasive than a relentless assault. Use phrasing like "I would prefer" rather than "You've got to" and strive for a happy resolution.

Capricorns are purposeful and like to use the minimum amount of energy to get things done. They're "no-frills" kind of people. But they are also so reserved that they feel foolish just saying anything, and Capricorns never like to feel foolish. If they want to chat, they'll come up with a reason to do so. Draw your husband out. He'll usually be happy to talk about his past, his family, or plans for the future. Once your Capricorn has opened up, however, you may wish he hadn't; he could be a notorious complainer. Try to get him to see the glass as half full rather than nearly empty!

You'll find your husband invaluable for help and advice on how to beat the system. These people know how to use the rules; they accept them as givens instead of rebelling or knuckling under. Then they turn them around and get them to work for them. A "catch-22" is the ultimate Capricorn challenge. If you're not sure how to file a tax return or what your next career move should be, ask your Capricorn. You'll find out everything you always wanted to know about corporate structure but were afraid to ask.

Capricorn actions and advice will be on the safe, conservative side, but it's always sound. You may think that your husband's change-saving jar idea is silly, but you'll also have to note that he slowly saved a bit of cash as a result—and actually enjoyed wrapping up those paper coin rolls! You might want him to handle the bills or investments. He'll do things reliably and on time.

Capricorns share an equal, if not greater, portion of the workload. They like to be useful and don't have a clue about working for a reward; the work is the reward. Your husband might take over and organize your bathroom remodeling project, planning who'll do what and scheduling when each task should be completed. Let him. He's good at it and loves it; it gives him a feeling of control.

Because a Capricorn is generally retiring, he won't actively seek to take the lead. But he'll try to take control by warning you about the importance of visiting your in-laws and being on time. If you're an independent type, this can be a little annoying. Capricorns worry about time and can be deadline crazy, but they usually don't miss deadlines. The rest of us can learn a thing or two about taking responsibility from these serious people.

You may be put off by his no-nonsense approach, but when there's a job to do, he can think of nothing else. He'll put in extra hours to pay for a new refrigerator, will always be sure your kids are looked after, and will maintain a secure and stable home life. You can depend on your Capricorn to be there when needed. He'll have a cool head in emergencies, and his take-charge attitude during these times can make you feel more secure.

So don't just shake your head at your quiet Capricorn, working diligently away in the corner when he could be out having fun. Entertain him, encourage him, and take his good advice. If you don't, he'll be chuckling all the way to the bank. You might as well tag along!

### Positives
Capricorn guys are looking for long-term relationships. They show up on time and don't break dates. They'll try to satisfy you and impress your family and friends.

### Negatives
He's not the most spontaneous person and could use some help in lightening up. He can be rigid and inflexible about his schedule. You may have to take a back seat to his goals and ambitions.

## YOUR CAPRICORN IN-LAWS

Capricorn in-laws are usually established, with stable lives, solid bank accounts, and good jobs. Some are status-conscious and may drive a Mercedes, but others prefer the simpler basics of life and love their Volkswagen Beetles.

It could take time to get to know this in-law. Typically, though, Capricorns loosen up a bit with age. Once they really know they're secure for the rest of their lives, they'll learn to lighten up and enjoy themselves...a little.

Capricorns are tied to the past and often attracted to history and the family. Your Capricorn in-law may wonder over "new-fangled gadgets" like smartphones or the Cloud, but will be the first to use them if they make life simpler or save money.

This sign may not make for the most generous of relatives. But Capricorns are usually committed to their children and may encourage traditions like holiday dinners and Fourth of July barbecues. You'll win points if you can join in the spirit of these festivities.

A Capricorn could appear cool, aloof, or even judgmental at times. But these in-laws appreciate connections. Give them plenty of notice for an invite over and treat them with respect, and you'll have a positive relationship for years to come.

## YOUR CAPRICORN MAID OF HONOR

Capricorn maids of honor are here to stay because they're so good at what they do. They need and want responsibility and will always do what's expected of them. This maid of honor has a job to do and will get it done. She'll inspire confidence and respect because she works hard. Her rule is unobtrusive but omnipresent. If you like, she'll take control of the whole operation, as she understands how to organize all the different elements of your wedding. Usually expert at timing and scheduling, she'll be sure each milestone—from the bridal shower to the honeymoon—is accomplished on time and without a fuss.

You'll find an often gentle, serious soul who won't take liberties with others and conducts business affairs on the up-and-up (it's too risky to take chances by breaking the rules!). She'll be willing to help out and offer advice on your wedding problems and struggles. Capricorns speak from experience. Many of them have taken on responsibility early in life and know how to get things done.

A Capricorn is reliable. You can count on her to hold your ring and have a mirror, makeup, and even extra stockings on hand if you need them. A Capricorn maid of honor loves tradition. She'll know how to handle marriage license requirements, the bridal registry, and the etiquette of writing thank-you notes.

Capricorns take everything seriously and may worry unnecessarily, so steer clear of doing things at the last minute. Your maid of honor will freak out if you postpone your fittings or deal with a less-than-responsive photographer. If you want a laid-back sidekick who improvises her way through the wedding process, this is not the woman for you!

Because Capricorns are naturally serious, your maid of honor may need time out, alone and away from all the goings-on. Be aware of this tendency and the fact that she's prey to dark moods at times. Try to inspire an upbeat attitude by reporting on a new vendor, money saved, or other positive wedding news. Activities and obligations are often good distractions for Capricorns, and your wedding could help if she's feeling low.

Some Capricorns might be stingy or money hungry, but the vast majority are simply modest in their spending. Your maid of honor is not overly generous but will pay what's appropriate. If you want to cut your budget without too many compromises, turn to this attendant; she'll work wonders.

If you let your Capricorn maid of honor get you organized, you can expect to have everything go like clockwork on your special day. You won't have to pin your dress together or worry that your hair will fall down. What more could you want? Remember, this is serious business! Your maid of honor will never forget.

# CHAPTER 23

# Aquarius

## (JANUARY 20–FEBRUARY 18)

The Aquarius man likes to surround himself with friends. He thinks for himself and does things his own way. Aquarians understand permanence but fiercely avoid relationship ruts. Aquarius men are rational. They like to make decisions based on objective, intelligent thought, and always try to avoid prejudice.

# YOUR AQUARIUS HUSBAND

Aquarians take their relationships in the same way: they are extremely "user-friendly." They're some of the easiest people to get along with as they strive for calm, friendly interaction. They're optimistic, idealistic, and usually kind. They live peacefully and are real individuals, so they'll respect your need to be independent and do your own thing too. Aquarian men are never possessive or jealous, and they value an intellectual connection.

Aquarians can be quirky, unusual people, and they often have strong friendships or involvements with social or community groups. You may at times feel like you're sharing your husband with the world at large. Let him be—he needs his space and will rebel if you try to rein him in. And don't worry: he can be "just friends" with other women too.

This zodiac sign won't get dull over the long haul. Just when you think he's settled into the routine of waking up every morning at 7:30 a.m. to read the paper, he'll start getting up at 7:00 a.m. to do yoga! Because he'll never get in too much of a rut, neither will you. Try to understand that this man may occasionally behave unpredictably and that he periodically does need change, though not necessarily always major change.

Aquarians can be real individualists, perhaps sporting orange ties, spiky hair, or retro sunglasses. No matter how conventional your husband may appear, you'll probably notice that extra earring or wild streak of red hair. Whatever it is, there'll be something that sets him apart, and he likes it that way. While Aquarians treat all people with the same respect and quiet understanding that they demand for themselves, they're die-hard individualists. That old 1970s adage "You do your thing and I do my thing" was probably dreamed up by an Aquarius. If you leave your husband enough space to "do his thing," you'll find him a very attractive partner.

Aquarians have a great intellectual curiosity and are thus excellent conversationalists and wonderful listeners. Your Aquarian is easy to talk to and be with. Friendship is an integral part of most of his relationships, including marriage. You'll often see something of the unique in his closest companions as well. He won't try to change people but instead sees the rest of us as interesting, charming characters in our own right. He generally won't get overly emotional or involved with people, and it's a rare Aquarian who will ever show signs of pettiness, jealousy, or vindictiveness.

If you want the objective view, ask your Aquarian husband. His calm, sane feedback can help you see a problem in a whole new light. Even tricky personal conflicts will not appear quite so sticky once an Aquarius has analyzed the situation with you. Aquarians always have unique perspectives and can help you to see things differently.

Though not particularly romantic or emotional, the Aquarius man can be very sexual. He may be intrigued to hear about your past relationships or discuss his own. Don't be afraid to mutually explore the *Kama Sutra* or try some sex toys just for the fun of it.

Heavy restrictions to an Aquarian's freedom can cause rebelliousness and absent-mindedness. These people need to do what they want, when they want, and where they want! If they're unhappy with what they consider a stifling atmosphere, they can become restless, unreliable, or depressed. It will be important in this relationship to have your own activities and interests and not expect to share absolutely everything with your husband.

Remember that people of this sign don't hold authorities or responsibilities as sacred. You cannot reason with an Aquarius by saying, "The IRS needs payment next week." Your husband believes that imposed structures and restrictions (like deadlines or having to answer to authority) are just that: imposed. The concepts of both "IRS" and "payment" are meaningless to an Aquarian who has his own individual code of ethics. These generally have to do with being loyal, fair, and just, but "To thine own self be true" is a top Aquarius priority. If being true to himself means he must sacrifice your (or the government's!) approval, so be it. Sound a little complex? It is. And you'll just have to get to know your Aquarius better to determine exactly what his own specific code of ethics is really all about.

Usually, though, logical appeals to his rational side can help out. "You did promise me you'd help" will work wonders, as Aquarians like to keep their word and try not to break promises. If, however, your husband has found that you coerced his promise through fraudulent means, he'll regard it as completely invalid!

Aquarians make worthy opponents, as they avoid getting worked up and are usually logical, even under pressure. It can be helpful to air, share, and discuss feelings, though you may have to nudge him a bit to do so. Since his convictions run deep, strive for win-win solutions or at least agree to disagree.

All Aquarians need to deliberate, to think long and hard, to see all sides of a question before taking action. They can occasionally appear helpless in emergencies because they don't have time to think things through the way they need to, and their systems can even "crash" due to excess stress or anxiety. Take your own initiative when you need quick decisive action.

Another result of the deliberate Aquarian thinking process is extreme obstinacy. Once your husband feels he's seen and analyzed every facet of a situation and has come to a logical conclusion, there may be no shaking him. Try telling a computer it's wrong! Yet there are ways around a stubborn Aquarius husband. You can appeal to everyone's right to an opinion or present new evidence. Most Aquarians will be open to these alternatives.

Like a computer, your Aquarian will help you to solve problems in new and intriguing ways and can be relied upon for fascinating and helpful information. Your husband has these positive attributes plus the great, rare ability to understand and tolerate all of humanity's foibles. Sounds like a wonderful combination!

### Positives

This guy wants a mate who's also a friend. He firmly believes in independence and will never force you to change your views, activities, or connections. He'll expect the same consideration from you.

### Negatives

He likes company, so you may have to hang with his gang when you'd rather be alone. He's understanding but not emotional, so might not respond to your strongest feelings.

## YOUR AQUARIUS IN-LAWS

Aquarius in-laws are not your typical parents. There will not be a lot of rules, regulations, or restrictions to learn or abide by. Aquarians function best in an environment of freedom and will grant independence to all relations.

He or she may be a die-hard Republican or a lifelong Democrat and won't hold back from airing those views. Aquarius in-laws may be passionate about UFOs, astrology, or computing. They're fond of discussion but also like to help. Don't worry: there's no obligation to an Aquarius, though you'll probably want to help these people out when they're in need. You'll know...they're not shy about asking.

Your in-law absorbs facts, ideas, situations, and personalities to come to logical conclusions. An Aquarius is very idealistic and might become angry and impatient with people who behave in an unfair manner. He or she may be involved with the school board, library, or chamber of commerce.

There's usually a humanitarian streak to most Aquarians, and they like to be involved with the community. There's also an eccentric side that may become more obvious as your in-law ages. Be tolerant. This person is an understanding individual first and foremost and can become a true friend if you want one. It won't take much effort!

## YOUR AQUARIUS MAID OF HONOR

Aquarian maids of honor fulfill their roles with easygoing natures and excellent decision-making capabilities. The best of them can even remain detached enough from the emotional chaos swirling around them to function as a sort of wise counselor.

If you need a role model, manager, leader, or organizer, you will not get it from an Aquarius, no matter how hard you try. These people dislike giving orders and are such individualists that they really don't understand exactly how to get someone to do something for them.

There are never any "power plays," ruthless tactics, or double-dealings with Aquarians. What you see is what you get: a thoughtful, intelligent, rational person who tries to do the right thing by others. An Aquarius won't prejudge attendants and will be curious to get to know your other friends and family. Aquarians love the excitement and variety of humanity. This maid of honor won't look down on someone who's divorced, juggling three partners, or even married to two! You can count on quiet understanding from this often-unconventional woman no matter what. You're her friend, so you're okay.

Aquarians try to maintain friendly relations with all and will rarely show evidence of temper or distress. The very sane Aquarian nature promotes good relationships and honest, intelligent business dealings at a time when these things may be essential.

An Aquarius likes to consider a wide range of options and realizes that everyone has a unique perspective. She'll help you consider the pros and cons of a hometown versus a destination wedding, or heels versus flats. She won't think you're "wrong" if the final decision doesn't reflect her input. Aquarians always grant others the right to their own views and outlook.

Turn to your maid of honor with complicated relationship issues. She's a good counselor and knows and understands how to deal effectively with others. You'll probably gain a more objective view, and there's wisdom in many Aquarian ideas, recommendations, and evaluations. Use them!

Don't be shy around this maid of honor. She'll let you know what she needs or wants but may not give you an answer to your queries right away. She needs to think over your request objectively and nonjudgmentally. At times absent-minded, she may need reminding more than once. Just don't rush! This sign needs time to deliberate.

One final note: never order this lady around! Aquarians may resent authority and will take this approach as your presumption to judge them. Try to be open, avoid rigidity, and go with the flow. If you can accept the unusual as part of your maid of honor's temperament, you'll do fine...and have fun in the process!

# CHAPTER 24

# Pisces

## (FEBRUARY 19–MARCH 20)

This guy is sweet, sensitive, and feeling. Your Pisces is a great listener and a total softie, though he can sometimes seem distant. Let him have some time alone to escape, pursue hobbies, or just wind down.

## YOUR PISCES HUSBAND

Who's that puppy dog you've brought home? The guy with the soulful gaze, happily trotting after you? It's a Pisces! This man is almost anti-macho. He's easy to please and will be very happy with whatever affection and treats you want to bestow on him. Try to be attentive. Though he'll rarely complain, he's a sensitive type who'll lap up all the warmth and support you can give.

Inside he's a true artist who wants a soul mate. He may be into poetry, art, music, or other simple pleasures. Of course, he might also drift into vegging out in front of the TV, so have a romantic movie ready to share with him. He'll respond to other mood-enhancers, too, like soft candlelight and champagne or pretending he's your knight in shining armor. Appeal to your Pisces fantasies by making him a playlist of his favorite ballads, dressing up like a sassy 1970s starlet, or sharing a hot tub together.

Your husband's kind, warm nature makes him a true intimate who'll always find time to listen to your problems. He's an idealist at heart who wants to see everyone love one another, and he's wise enough not to try to change others. Tolerance is a key word for Pisceans. While they always give of themselves emotionally, they rarely make demands.

Generally, Pisceans have good senses of humor, and some are genuine jokesters. In a positive mood they know how to have a good time and how to make others happy. Genial, sociable, and likeable, they'll go along with suggestions and often love going out.

The day-to-day practicalities of life might well be things that your husband doesn't relate to easily, though, as he's caught up in his own inner world. You may need to remind him not to leave his socks on the floor! If he knows how to direct and use his personal strengths, that's great. If, on the other hand, he's got a job that demands deadlines or has a competitive atmosphere, your Piscean will be out of place. He could even appear to be a misfit in certain situations, as he can't really relate to acquisitiveness, power struggles, and "moving up" the way most people can.

Your Pisces husband needs time alone to relax and recharge. When under stress he'll retreat into your den, a secluded corner, or even his own head. He can be moody and is a very empathetic individual. A sad story might bring a lump to his throat, and sharp words or unconcern from others can depress him.

A Piscean may also not admit he's upset and will sometimes avoid talking about what's bothering him. If this is the case, gentle nudging toward some activity that he enjoys may be in order. The best way to live with a Pisces who's feeling low is to show your care and concern and offer your encouragement in any way possible. This man will often turn down help in a self-effacing way, but you might just get him a cup of coffee or a snack to show you care. Or do any little thing that you know he'll appreciate. A positive boost like this could be just the thing he needs to turn his spirits around.

Pisceans often view the world through rose-colored glasses and like to think that everyone is as well-intentioned and good-natured as they are. They see things in terms of moods, feelings, and images. A Piscean may be misunderstood because of his communication of impressions rather than facts. He can also be difficult to pin down because he doesn't relate to specifics well. Because of his acute sensitivity, he may not always "tell it like it is." Your husband might tell you what you want to hear, what won't hurt you, or what he feels will have the most positive effect on you. With this emphasis, there can be a straying from "hard reality" as more practical or logical people understand it. You may have to back up key communiqués from your husband with input from other, more objective friends or relatives to get a specific, more accurate picture. Don't be surprised, though, if various companions report conflicting information from your Pisces mate. They were probably given the same impressions and came to different logical conclusions on their own.

Pisceans are the last people of the zodiac to understand schedules or deadlines. In their inner lives, time is not significant. Your husband will proceed at his own rate and may need outside mobilization to pick up the pace. He can forget deadlines, promises, and commitments. Getting a Pisces to agree to sign papers at the bank at some point in the future and actually getting him to do it might be difficult. He'll leave when you tell him to, run into a friend on the way, stop for a beer, and forget all about his errand! You're better off sharing a project with your Pisces, as these people are usually responsive. If you go with him to the bank, you should have better results.

Pressuring a Pisces may get you the opposite of what you want. Anger can cause him to shut down or even disappear for a while. Try instead to channel your energy into an appeal to his naturally sympathetic side.

Get your Pisces husband to give imaginative input. He has many ideas and opinions and makes a great contributor to brainstorming sessions about kitchen design, vacations, or buying a home. His ideas exist for their own sake and are not censored due to practicality or other limitations. All Pisceans have their own unique viewpoints, which are often quite different from those of the rest of us.

In dividing tasks, remember that Pisceans gravitate toward creative work and love to interact with others if they don't have to be aggressive. Your help in reminding your Pisces husband of important events and obligations will ensure that he's available for shared tasks, activities, and responsibilities. You may have to take the lead. Weekly or even daily reviews can have a good effect by updating and enthusing your Pisces on a regular basis. But don't be too forceful with deadlines or your Pisces will evade and escape you!

Show emotional support and concern when you can. Your compassion and understanding of your Pisces man will be returned with the great trust, dedication, and understanding of a person whose still waters run very deep and who gives you his all when the chips are down.

### Positives

A Pisces man can worship you like a goddess. He makes no demands but is always there to please you. He'll do anything for those he loves.

### Negatives

Who knows what goes on inside this moody guy's head? He can hide away when upset. He could get addicted to food, drinking, or even drugs to escape his problems.

## YOUR PISCES IN-LAWS

Pisces is the last sign of the zodiac and probably the most complex. A Pisces can be joyful, self-sacrificing, or a lost soul—sometimes a bit of all three—and these characteristics will be clearer with age.

Pisces in-laws will easily welcome you into the family and make you feel a comfortable part of their domestic circle. They may have weathered emotional crises, illness, or other life challenges and come out stronger. They're good listeners, as they usually understand exactly what you're going through. Most will shy away from interfering in your personal affairs, but they'll be pleased to come over for dinner, go out to a movie, or invite you to swim in their pool on a hot day.

A quality that's characteristic of Pisces people is their lack of boundaries. You'll have to see how this manifests; it may be an unlimited love for your husband, dedication to a charitable cause, or trust in a higher power. Or Pisceans could potentially be food or substance abusers, mysterious personalities, or even reclusive.

Take advantage of their instincts, talents, and creative ideas. But remember that no Pisces can give you something you don't already have.

## YOUR PISCES MAID OF HONOR

The Pisces maid of honor is good-hearted and likeable, a human being first and foremost. She'll be genuinely helpful and attentive to your needs and will always take time out to listen to what you've got to say—the only problem is that nothing may ever be done about it! These people often learn to live with less-than-ideal conditions and could counsel you to do the same. "That's just the way things are" is a truly Piscean statement.

This maid of honor is a good friend, however. She's someone to talk to and share problems with who'll stick with you through the highs and lows of your wedding planning. She'll be generous with both time and money, even if she has little of either. She'll encourage a friendly, dormitory-like atmosphere with the bridesmaids. She's a talented, sensitive type and is really not cut out for the harsh or aggressive side of life.

Your maid of honor acts primarily on emotion and instinct. She doesn't like to offend anyone and so may be loath to offer criticism. She might tell you what you want to hear, just to make you feel better. So get another opinion if you really want to know whether that dress makes your butt look too big.

Pisceans are often creative or "idea" people who need to have a structure surrounding them in order to function best. If you're organized, efficient, and reliable, you could be the perfect foil for your Pisces maid of honor, who'll eagerly help you dream up themes, suggest favors, and offer fashion ideas. If you can tune in to her wavelength, you'll do fine.

Literal-minded or detail-oriented people may be frustrated with what they see as Piscean inattention to important facts. It's all in how you look at things. Remembering that your Pisces maid of honor may be looking out from inside a fishbowl can help.

At times bright and sociable, the Pisces maid of honor can be emotional and will withdraw when down or upset. It's best not to intrude at these times. If you must, be gentle and kind and keep your own spirits up; it could have a beneficial effect on her.

Don't expect your Pisces maid of honor to solve all the problems in your wedding planning. A Pisces will often avoid open conflict and is not always the best at mediating disputes. But she'll be there to support you, listen to your problems, and do whatever she can to help.

Pisceans can be delightful to work with, and they'll often create a little bit of that idealized world they'd so like to live in. It can be fun in the Pisces fishbowl for you too!

# APPENDIX:
## Your Wedding Day

## CHOOSING YOUR WEDDING DATE

People have birth dates, corporations have birth dates, and even buildings do (think about ground-breaking or ribbon-cutting ceremonies). The start of any enterprise or relationship also has a birth date and a horoscope all its own. Your relationship may have begun on the day you met, your first date, or your first kiss. But there's one day you'll never forget: your wedding.

Your wedding day is more important than other relationship milestones because it represents a commitment. You're exchanging vows before your family and closest friends, and an official has authorized your union. It's also legally binding, making it more significant: you share the rights, privileges, and responsibilities that married couples enjoy. If you live together and decide to call it quits, you can go your separate ways. If you're married and choose to divorce, legal procedures must be followed.

A marriage is much more than simply saying, "I do." It may represent a spiritual bond, a joining of opposites or a promise to share your future together. You're truly connected as you've never been before.

When a professional astrologer chooses a favorable date and time, it might highlight a focus on children, help firm up finances, or keep your connection strong. It cannot guarantee a happy marriage. And your basic compatibility and maturity have more to do with making your relationship last than the actual wedding date itself.

But choosing a good wedding day gives you an edge. And who can't use that in these days of emotional complexity and frequent separations? Forewarned is forearmed: if you know what to expect, you'll be more relaxed and more likely to handle any bumps in the road with patience and a positive attitude. A good wedding date also gives you better odds that the ceremony and party will go smoothly.

Astrologers have been choosing wedding dates for what seems like an eternity. Ancient Roman astrologers, twelfth-century Jewish mystics, advisers to Turkish sultans, and seventeenth-century English consultants all selected lucky dates for their clients, family members, and even themselves. In many Asian countries, like India, China, and Japan, it's still customary to consult an astrologer for a lucky wedding date. As astrology gained popularity in the West in the 1960s and 1970s, more wedding dates were chosen astrologically, and the trend continues today. Surprisingly enough, the basic rules governing this over 2,000-year-old tradition have remained virtually unchanged throughout the centuries.

These time-honored tips can help any bride choose a wedding date on her own. The influences of Mercury retrograde, Venus retrograde, and eclipses may be challenging, but they're easily avoided, as you'll see in the sections that follow.

What if you've already chosen a date that has one of these unusual influences? Awareness of possible issues is always helpful, and there are ways to work productively with the planetary energies. Longer term and more committed couples will no doubt do better with potentially problematic astrological signatures, as they're already used to working at their relationship and know how to adapt and adjust to one another's needs.

## WATCH OUT!: MERCURY RETROGRADE

Computers crash, texts are lost in cyberspace, appointments are missed, and cashiers hand out the wrong change. All this and more happens when Mercury is retrograde. Why? About three times a year Mercury, the planetary ruler of communications and counting, apparently backtracks or reverses its path in the sky. All kinds of confusion and miscommunication can result. The most famous example of a Mercury retrograde mix-up is the 2000 US presidential election, where there wasn't a clear winner and pollsters had to recount votes and turn the decision over to the Supreme Court.

How can this affect your wedding or marriage? There may be mix-ups on a day when you least need them. The caterer serves up 200 plates rather than 150, the limo driver loses your address, or your out-of-town guests get on the wrong train. It's best to avoid these dates if you can. If you can't, be prepared for little glitches and consider choosing an attendant in charge of mishaps! At the very worst, Mercury retrograde could cause you to garble your vows, trip on your train, or even change your mind. On rare occasions, the very legality of the ceremony comes into question.

If you'll have Mercury retrograde in your wedding horoscope, you may simply have to work harder at communicating with your spouse. Keep your appliances in repair, get your car tuned up on a regular basis, and talk, talk, talk!

Mercury retrograde can also indicate reaffirming vows, so it's appropriate for couples in a second ceremony or those recommitting to one another. It's also a classic placement for marriages of couples who've already lived together, as they are now making a greater commitment to the relationship.

Mercury is retrograde on the following dates:

## 2019
March 5–March 27, 2019
July 7–August 1, 2019
October 31–November 19, 2019

## 2020
February 17–March 9, 2020
June 18–July 11, 2020
October 14–November 2, 2020

## 2021
January 30–February 20, 2021
May 29–June 21, 2021
September 27–October 17, 2021

## 2022
January 14–February 3, 2022
May 10–June 2, 2022
September 10–October 1, 2022
December 29, 2022–January 17, 2023

## 2023
April 21–May 14, 2023
August 23–September 14, 2023
December 13, 2023–January 1, 2024

## 2024

April 2–April 24, 2024
August 5–August 27, 2024
November 26–December 14, 2024

## 2025

March 15–April 6, 2025
July 18–August 10, 2025
November 9–November 28, 2025

## 2026

February 26–March 19, 2026
June 29–July 22, 2026
October 24–November 12, 2026

## 2027

February 9–March 2, 2027
June 10–July 3, 2027
October 7–October 27, 2027

## 2028

January 24–February 13, 2028
May 21–June 13, 2028
September 19–October 10, 2028

## 2029

January 7–January 26, 2029
May 2–May 24, 2029
September 2–September 24, 2029
December 22, 2029–January 10, 2030

## 2030

April 13–May 5, 2030
August 16–September 7, 2030
December 6–December 24, 2030

## A DIFFERENT KIND OF RELATIONSHIP: VENUS RETROGRADE

Venus also goes retrograde, though less often than Mercury. It appears to turn backward in its path through the sky about five times in eight years, for a period of about six weeks at a time. Traditional astrology suggests avoiding Venus retrograde for a wedding date, since Venus is the planet of love. Its energies can be weaker or its influence more passive than it ordinarily might be. Some astrologers feel that the Venusian energies are internalized or turned inward, making it tougher to connect or share emotions. Others have found that this placement can add emotional complexity to the marriage, perhaps from the couple's previous relationships or children from an earlier union, for example.

Despite many astrologers warning against this placement, just consider: could *all* the couples married in a six-week period have problems? Definitely not. Venus retrograde is just another notable influence to consider. If you've already set a date with Venus retrograde, it's important to stay in touch with your feelings and make an extra effort to share them with your spouse. This can take both time and patience.

Venus also relates to pleasure, enjoyment, and harmonious social relations. Interactions become more complex with Venus retrograde. Legal affairs might be complicated. Or the self-indulgent side of Venus may be exaggerated, resulting in overeating, drinking too much, or overspending.

Venus also relates to beauty, money, and possessions. Major purchases, investments, or home decorating should always be carefully considered with this placement in a wedding chart. A couple's sense of beauty might be unusual, or they may disagree about home design, for example, though Venus retrograde does favor redecorating.

Venus will be retrograde on the following dates:

- May 13–June 24, 2020
- December 19, 2021–January 28, 2022
- July 23–September 3, 2023
- March 2–April 12, 2025
- October 3–November 13, 2026
- May 10–June 21, 2028
- December 16, 2029–January 25, 2030

## A WILD RIDE: THE INFLUENCE OF ECLIPSES

Eclipses have a bad reputation in astrological lore. They're said to bring emotional instability, discontent, and even disaster. Ancient Babylonian cuneiform tablets shout warnings of the death of kings and the destruction of temples under their influence. Sixth-century B.C. Chinese classics see the phenomenon as "ugly" and "abnormal." Bible commentators have linked not only the death of Christ but also the Great Flood to eclipses. Shakespeare had both Gloucester in *King Lear* and Othello blame their problems on them too. And Nancy Reagan's astrologer persuaded the president to delay announcing his second term candidacy until January of 1984: there were two eclipses the previous December.

The influence of eclipses may be exaggerated, as most of us regularly survive about one total solar eclipse per year. But catastrophic prophecies continue. One can understand why: for all our scientific understanding, there's still something spooky about the Sun being darkened and the temperature dropping in the middle of the day, or the Moon turning blood red—a bit of primeval chaos in the midst of the information age.

It's best to avoid eclipses for your wedding date if you can. In fact, you should plan to avoid ten days before to at least three days after an eclipse for best results. Eclipses suggest high emotions, oversensitivity, and even disagreements. They may also result in eventful, high-profile, or much-publicized weddings. Wedding day eclipses are probably easier on more mature or longer-term couples who've already established a solid relationship.

If you plan to be married near an eclipse, try to control your emotions and feelings. All couples deal with difficulties in life, so make an effort to take things in stride and don't exaggerate your problems. Consciously address frustrations with the home, family, or in-laws in a calm and rational manner. Focus on the positive and celebrate what you share.

Some couples simply prefer a high-adventure, somewhat unpredictable, and emotionally charged lifestyle. If this sounds like you, you have nothing to fear from an eclipse—it'll give you all you crave! But if you prefer harmony, security, and stability, you should try to avoid dates ten days before to three days after the eclipses.

Eclipses often come in pairs separated by about two weeks. They occur on the following dates:

- **2019:** January 6, January 21, July 2, July 16, December 26
- **2020:** January 10, June 5, June 21, July 5, November 30, December 14
- **2021:** May 26, June 10, November 19, December 4
- **2022:** April 30, May 16, October 25, November 8
- **2023:** April 20, May 5, October 14, October 28
- **2024:** March 25, April 8, September 18, October 2
- **2025:** March 14, March 29, September 7, September 21
- **2026:** February 17, March 3, August 12, August 28
- **2027:** February 6, February 20, July 18, August 2, August 17
- **2028:** January 12, January 26, July 6, July 22, December 31
- **2029:** January 14, June 12, June 26, July 11, December 5, December 20
- **2030:** June 1, June 15, November 25, December 9

# Bibliography

Campion, Nicholas. *The Book of World Horoscopes* (Wellingborough, England: Thorsons Publishing Group, 1988).

Cramer, Diane. *Managing Your Health & Wellness* (Woodbury, MN: Llewellyn Publications, 2006).

George, Llewellyn. *Llewellyn's New A-to-Z Horoscope Maker and Interpreter* (St. Paul, MN: Llewellyn Publications, 2003).

Holden, James Herschel. *A History of Horoscopic Astrology* (Tempe, AZ: American Federation of Astrologers, Inc., 1996).

Michelsen, Neil F. *The American Ephemeris for the 21st Century* (San Diego, CA: ACS Publications, 1992).

Michelsen, Neil F. *Tables of Planetary Phenomena* (San Diego, CA: ACS Publications, 1990).

Penfield, Marc. *Horoscopes of the Western Hemisphere* (San Diego, CA: ACS Publications, 1984).

Polkosnik, Greg. *Cosmically Chic* (Kansas City, MO: Andrews McMeel Publishing, 2000).

Stellas, Constance. *The Astrology Gift Guide* (New York, NY: Signet, 2002).

The Flower Expert. "Flowers & Astrology." www.theflowerexpert.com/content/miscellaneous/flowers-and-astrology.

Virtue, Doreen, and Judith Lukomski. *Crystal Therapy* (Carlsbad, CA: Hay House, Inc., 2005).

# Index

## A

Aquarius
  attendants, 213–14
  beauty tips for, 118–19
  bride, 115–25
  characteristics of, 115–17, 208–12
  colors for, 120
  date ideas for, 121
  flowers for, 120
  gemstones for, 120
  groom, 208–12
  honeymoons for, 120
  in-laws, 212–13
  long-term relationships, 121–24
  love for, 121
  maid of honor, 213–14
  positives/negatives, 212
  sex for, 121
  sharing thoughts with, 124–25
  stress-free tips for, 118
  wedding ceremony for, 119–20
  wedding planning for, 116–17
Aries
  attendants, 143–44
  beauty tips for, 15–16
  bride, 12–21
  characteristics of, 12–14, 138–42
  colors for, 17
  date ideas for, 18
  flowers for, 16
  gemstones for, 16
  groom, 138–42
  honeymoons for, 17
  in-laws, 142–43

  long-term relationships, 18–20
  love for, 17–18
  maid of honor, 143–44
  positives/negatives, 142
  sex for, 17–18
  sharing thoughts with, 20–21
  stress-free tips for, 15
  wedding ceremony for, 16–17
  wedding planning for, 13–14
Astrology
  benefits of, 7–8
  for bride, 7–8, 11–135
  for groom, 7–8, 137–221
  for wedding day, 7–8, 222–30
Attendants
  Aquarius, 213–14
  Aries, 143–44
  Cancer, 164–65
  Capricorn, 206–7
  Gemini, 157–58
  Leo, 171–72
  Libra, 185–86
  Pisces, 220–21
  Sagittarius, 199–200
  Scorpio, 192–93
  Taurus, 150–51
  Virgo, 178–79
  Zodiac signs for, 143–221

## B

Beauty tips
  for Aquarians, 118–19
  for Ariens, 15–16
  for Cancerians, 46–47

232

## Z

# About the Author

Karen Christino was the astrologer for *Modern Bride* and *Your Prom* magazines for ten years, and has written horoscope columns for *Glamour*, *Cosmopolitan*, and *Life & Style* magazines. Her seven books on astrology include *Foreseeing the Future: Evangeline Adams and Astrology in America* and *Regal Brides: The Astrology of Five American Women and their Royal Marriages*. She has a BA from Colgate University and lives in New York City with her husband. Visit her website at KarenChristino.com.